Modern Poetry

Studies in Practical Criticism

Modern Poetry
Studies in Practical Criticism

C. B. COX & A. E. DYSON

LONDON
EDWARD ARNOLD (PUBLISHERS) LTD

First published, 1963
Reprinted 1963
Reprinted 1967

Printed in Great Britain by
The Camelot Press Ltd., London and Southampton

CONTENTS

ACKNOWLEDGEMENTS

THE Authors and Publisher wish to acknowledge the kind permission given by Jonathan Cape, Ltd. to reprint *O Dreams, O Destinations* (from *Word Over All*) by C. Day Lewis; Chatto & Windus, Ltd. to reprint *Futility* by Wilfred Owen; J. M. Dent & Sons, Ltd. to reprint *Fern Hill* by Dylan Thomas; Faber & Faber, Ltd. to reprint *Marina* by T. S. Eliot, *The Landscape Near An Aerodrome* by Stephen Spender, *Snow* by Louis Mac-Neice, *Poem For Elsa* by Michael Roberts, *The Horses* by Edwin Muir (all from *Collected Poems*), *Spain 1937* by W. H. Auden (from *Collected Shorter Poems*), *The Casualty* by Ted Hughes (from *The Hawk in the Rain*) and *Considering the Snail* by Thom Gunn; Faber & Faber, Ltd. and Mrs. H. Thomas to reprint *The Signpost* by Edward Thomas; Rupert Hart-Davis, Ltd. to reprint *A Blackbird Singing* by R. S. Thomas; International Authors N. V. to reprint *Vanity* by Robert Graves (from *Collected Poems* published by Cassell & Co., Ltd.); Macmillan & Co., Ltd. to reprint *After a Journey* by Thomas Hardy, *On the Death of a Murderer* by John Wain (from *Weep Before God*); Macmillan & Co., Ltd. and Mrs. Yeats to reprint *Easter 1916* by W. B. Yeats; Laurence Pollinger, Ltd. and the Estate of the late Mrs. Frieda Lawrence to reprint *Bavarian Gentians* by D. H. Lawrence; The Marvell Press to reprint *At Grass* by Philip Larkin (from *The Less Deceived*); The Society of Authors to reprint *The Listeners* by Walter de la Mare.

INTRODUCTION

1 *The beginnings of practical criticism*

When the Cambridge English Tripos was started in 1917, most critics of poetry wrote in a highly generalised, metaphorical style. The reviews in *The Times Literary Supplement* inclined towards gossip, and were full of description and unspecific praise. They used phrases such as 'golden verse', 'pure tender spirit', or 'his mind was like the wide world dreaming of things to come'. Behind this style was the assumption that literature was a thing of beauty, a product of moonlight and exaltation, and that poetry should be a gateway into the ideal.

In *The Muse Unchained* (1958), E. M. W. Tillyard has described how in the post-1918 period the teachers at Cambridge wanted to supplant this imprecise laudatory criticism by something more rigorous. Particularly influential was I. A. Richards, whose famous book, *Practical Criticism*, was published in 1929. Richards had been trained as a philosopher, and took a First in Moral Science in 1915. When he was a student, the most influential teacher of philosophy at Cambridge was G. E. Moore, who was one of the fathers of modern linguistic analysis. The interest of modern philosophers, such as A. J. Ayer, in the meaning of words runs parallel with developments in literary criticism. Richards learnt from Moore to scrutinise apparently simple statements, and to consider their various shades of meaning. He applied these techniques to imaginative literature, and gradually moved towards the conception of critical analysis which is current today. When in 1926 the English Tripos was extended, practical criticism established itself as an essential part of the examination. In the ensuing years, close scrutiny of literary texts was introduced as a normal part of many university courses. It has become increasingly popular in schools, and questions such as 'Analyse the technique and meaning of the following poem' have set hearts palpitating in both 'O' and 'A' level candidates.

The word 'analysis' was used by the Cambridge critics in a new way. They were not concerned with orthodox rules of grammar, but with an attempt to describe precisely the imaginative effects of literature. They were more interested than most of the great critics of the past in close study of particular texts. In the 1930's the great practitioners were F. R. Leavis, William Empson and L. C. Knights, whose brilliant and controversial analyses made the technique world famous. Their influence has dominated much of the best English and American criticism of succeeding decades; but recently many influential teachers have had second thoughts. Both Helen Gardner and C. S. Lewis have vigorously attacked the practical effects of this method; critics such as Donald Davie and Frank Kermode have challenged some of its basic assumptions. Knowledge of the history of practical criticism and of the current argument is essential if the technique is to be used effectively today.

2   The assumptions of practical criticism

The Cambridge teachers were much influenced by Freud, and felt that just as human action is a product of hidden motives, so the richer type of poetry contains underlying meanings. The early practitioners of analysis were adept at discovering subtle implications, of which the poet himself was probably unaware; William Empson's *Seven Types of Ambiguity* (1930) is a supreme example of this type of approach. He tells us that 'Wordsworth frankly had no inspiration other than his use, when a boy, of the mountains as a totem or father-substitute, and Byron only at the end of his life, in the first cantos of *Don Juan* in particular, escaped from the infantile incest-fixation upon his sister which was till then all he had got to say.'

Just as influential as Freud, however, was T. S. Eliot, whose critical essays had a revolutionary effect in Cambridge. The writings of F. R. Leavis and his co-operators in the journal, *Scrutiny*, which was started in 1932, were in large part an attempt to apply Eliot's ideas in practice. Two of Eliot's theories in particular were of great influence on the analysis of poetry. In his essay 'The Metaphysical Poets' (1921), he described the 'dissociation of sensibility' which he believed took place about 1650 among English writers. And in his essay on *Hamlet* (1919), he talked about the need for an 'objective correlative' if a writer is to realise his experiences in a series of words. Both essays were reprinted in *Selected Essays* (1932). It is these two concepts in particular that since 1950 have aroused so much controversy.

For Eliot, a great poem is the product of a unified sensibility. In the poetry of Donne for instance, we find thought and emotion working together:

> Tennyson and Browning are poets, and they think; but they do not feel their thought as immediately as the odour of a rose. A thought to Donne was an experience; it modified his sensibility. When a poet's mind is perfectly equipped for its work, it is constantly amalgamating disparate experience; the ordinary man's experience is chaotic, irregular, fragmentary. The latter falls in love, or reads Spinoza, and these two experiences have nothing to do with each other, or with the noise of the typewriter or the smell of cooking; in the mind of the poet these experiences are always forming new wholes.

Eliot argues that after the early seventeenth century this unique quality of the great poet was lost: 'a dissociation of sensibility set in, from which we have never recovered.' Poets either discoursed about feelings, so diluting their content, or did not think sufficiently about their own overflowing emotions. They offered only a part of what makes the greatest poetry. Eliot's aim was to make his own verse a product of the unified sensibility; and his followers at Cambridge believed that poetry could help them to partake of this unique, rich consciousness of the artist. For Leavis and his followers, analysis was not merely a technique for precise description of literature, but a process whereby the reader could 'cultivate awareness', and grow towards the unified sensibility. Analysis was necessary because a poem resulted from a complex of associated feelings and thoughts. A great poem was not a simple, forceful statement of some well-known experience, 'What oft was thought, but ne'er so well express'd', but a profoundly original creation only fully comprehended after close textual analysis. Because of these attitudes, the practical critic spent his time discovering complexities, ambiguities and multiplications of meaning. He was attracted to irony and wit, because a poem with these qualities offers different layers of effect for interpretation. Long, discursive poems, such as *Paradise Lost*, which depend for much of their organisation on rational analysis, were undervalued, and the critics tended to treat all poems, and even plays and novels, as akin to lyric poetry in their structure of imagery.

In the first issue of *Scrutiny*, the sponsors wrote in their manifesto that 'there is a necessary relationship between the quality of the individual's response to art and his general fitness for a humane existence.' Modern society had been corrupted by urbanisation, the pressures of economic competition and the misuse of advertising; in this fallen world, the literary critic was a member of a small élite. Through his contact with literature, he was aware of a rich tradition lost to the vast majority of his contemporaries. Through analyses of poems, he achieved knowledge of the subtleties and riches of the unified sensibility. This theory of the moral value of literature, outlined rather crudely and simply here, has been the source of many of the bitter conflicts about practical criticism. For its practitioners, literary analysis was not an academic exercise, but the key to mature values.

Eliot's definitions of the unified sensibility derive from the French symbolists, such as Mallarmé, who influenced T. E.

Hulme, Ezra Pound and the 'Imagist' school in pre-Great War England. For these writers, the substance of a poem was the image and its resonances. The imagination offered a type of knowledge superior to that of rational analysis, superior to the empirical discoveries of science. The image in a poem gave the reader a moment of illumination beyond normal apprehension, and so introduced him to a kind of sensibility not to be found in everyday living. Frank Kermode has described these influences in great detail in *The Romantic Image* (1957), and shown that this emphasis on the image has had a very considerable effect on techniques of literary analysis. The student has been taught to look mainly at the various effects of individual images, and then to consider the interrelationship of images throughout the poem. Many analyses of poems have paid no attention to rhyme, conventions of genre, or syntax, but have concentrated upon the complex pattern of imagery. The implication has been that a poem has an organisation of its own, based upon the image, and that ordinary grammatical structure is of comparatively small importance. Eliot's *The Waste Land*, of course, demonstrates this conception of linked images. Such analyses of imagery have been applied successfully to the poetry of the metaphysicals, or to Hopkins, for example, but they have had little to say about the typical Elizabethan sonnet or song, or about the structure of the long poems of Milton, Dryden or Pope.

This emphasis on the image leads to Eliot's definition of the 'objective correlative'. In his essay on *Hamlet*, he claims that Shakespeare has been unable to find a chain of events adequate to express the emotions of his main character. The play is an artistic failure because Shakespeare could not fully transform the revenge play so that it would express the disgust and bafflement of Hamlet's experience:

The only way of expressing emotion in the form of art is by finding an "objective correlative"; in other words, a set of objects, a situation, a chain of events which shall be the formula of that *particular* emotion; such that when the external facts, which must terminate in sensory experience, are given, the emotion is immediately evoked.

Eliot's interpretation of the objective correlative illustrates his view that experience cannot be adequately described in rational language, but can be fully expressed only when realised in images. In a play, the 'images' are the situations, and the relationships between the characters, as well as the actual pictures in the words themselves.

From these views of the dissociation of sensibility and the objective correlative, F. R. Leavis derives much of the critical language he uses in his analyses of poems. He talks repeatedly of 'significance', and tries to assess how far the poem expresses a unified sensibility; and he considers how far the significance is 'realised' in the words. 'Significance' and 'realisation' are words he uses repeatedly; and the Pelican Guides to English Literature, written mainly by his followers, are full of this kind of language. Through detailed analysis of poetry, and particularly of imagery, the reader assimilates the riches of tradition, expressed in the maturity of literary evaluation.

3 *The reaction against the Cambridge method of practical criticism*

From its earliest days, the Cambridge school had to face hostile and angry criticism. The philologists insisted that the English Tripos did not offer a true discipline of the mind, and that the study of language was an essential part in any course of literature. This type of objection continues, and recently philologists have turned to the new science of linguistics to counter the Cambridge emphasis on literary appreciation.

More important, some of the most influential teachers of literature have argued that the method achieves unfortunate results. In 'The Academic Study of English Literature' (*The*

Critical Quarterly, Vol. I, No. 2), Helen Gardner argues that the purpose of teaching English is not to produce critics:

> I would hope that my pupils' taste and power of judgement would grow by familiarity with great writers, and that their general powers of discrimination would be sharpened, in the sense that they would be better able to distinguish sense from nonsense, facts from opinions, established facts from well-supported hypotheses, and that they would have learned to read carefully and to write lucidly. In other words, I hope that they would emerge as educated persons, able to conduct arguments, collect relevant information, and scrutinise their own opinions as well as those of other people. I should hope that they would be scrupulous in not talking about a subject without making a proper enquiry into what is known about it. But I do not believe that the study of English literature at the university can, of itself, make people more capable of original and significant judgements. If criticism is to be equated with 'evaluation' and the critic is the person with the power to recognise the excellent, distinguish it from the merely pleasing, and reject the meretricious, I have not found, nor should I expect to find, critical authority to have any connection with whether or not the critic read English as an undergraduate.

This denies the basic contention of *Scrutiny* writers that literary analysis gives special insights to its practitioners. Both Helen Gardner and C. S. Lewis have pointed out that a student can be taught a technique of analysis, and do well in examinations, without any real appreciation of poetry whatsoever. He can learn how to talk about the meanings of an image, and about the relationships between images, even though he has no liking for verse. Teachers in schools and universities have learnt to help students to pass examinations in this way, and so the exercise itself is losing its educational value. Also, C. S. Lewis doubts whether it is wise to impose judgement on a pupil at school whose taste is still not mature. In order to pass examinations, a student must point out why one poet is better than another, why Hopkins is greater than Bridges, for example, when in fact he may well prefer the lesser poet. A young reader matures his taste by passing through enthusiasms for writers such as Christina Rossetti, Galsworthy and Hugh Walpole; and the techniques of analysis force established judgements down his throat at too early an age. Many teachers would agree that such bad effects are very possible, and that the habit of analysis may well produce wrong attitudes to poetry. The examinee who discovers the most subtleties and ambiguities in a poem is judged the most original, and may get the most marks. Complex poetry thus becomes over-valued at the expense of the simple and direct. A poet such as Herrick has received little attention recently because his verse offers comparatively few rewards to the analyst. At a recent examiners' meeting to prepare Finals papers, R. S. Thomas's delightful poem, 'A Blackbird Singing', was put forward as suitable for an analysis question; it was rejected because it was not difficult enough. The dangers illustrated by this story are obvious enough.

In addition to these practical objections, there have been a number of searching enquiries into the attitudes towards imagery accepted by practical critics. Of these the two most important are Donald Davie's *Articulate Energy* (1955), and Frank Kermode's *Romantic Image* (1957). Davie's book is closely argued, and does not make easy reading, but it is one of the most important critical books of the 1950's. Davie challenges Eliot's definition of the objective correlative. In Davie's view, language achieves its effects by a variety of means, and one of the most important is by the use of orthodox syntax. He discerns two prevalent attitudes towards language. On the one hand, the writer, through syntax, imposes order upon his material, and shows the way in which the conscious mind can perceive harmonious relationships between apparently disparate fields of experience. Language is thought of as an instrument of articulation, a way of establishing relationships like the harmonies of music or the equations of algebra. The second attitude, popular among the poets of the 1920's, comes from a loss of faith in syntax. For the imagists and their followers, language is trustworthy only when it is broken down into units of isolated words, when it abandons any attempt at large-scale, rational articulation. The poet is an isolated man, achieving sympathy with others only in momentary flashes, and expressing himself in the unit of the image. In the seventeenth and eighteenth centuries, poets acted on the assumption that syntax in poetry should carry a weight of poetic meaning; in the twentieth century, poets have tended to act on the opposite assumption. For them, a poem has organic form, often dependent on the structure of images, and when syntactical forms are retained they carry little weight.

Davie argues that 'systems of syntax are part of the heritable property of past civilisation, and to hold firm to them is to be traditional in the best and most important sense . . . the abandonment of syntax testifies to a failure of the poet's nerve, a loss of confidence in the intelligible structure of the conscious mind, and the validity of its activity'. Eliot's theory of the objective correlative indicates a loss of faith in conceptual thought, and much subsequent analysis of poetry is grounded on the delusion that what cannot be imaged cannot be conceived. In fact, abstract language can often be more concrete, more adequate as an articulation of experience, than imagery. Coleridge himself believed that conceptual thinking outstripped thinking in images. One of Leavis's favourite examples of 'concrete' imagery is Keats's 'moss'd cottage trees'. Such imagery is by no means necessarily a more penetrating account of experience than the rational descriptive language of the philosopher.

Davie's aim is to show the inadequacy of the symbolist and post-symbolist tradition both in poetry and criticism. Critics such as F. R. Leavis lay great stress on the poet's task in breaking down the reader's 'stock responses', in getting through or behind the existing conventions. The poet's task is to be faithful to his unique experience, and to read his verse the individual must go through a period of strenuous training and rehabilitation. In contrast, Davie believes that words should be part of a sort of contract entered into tacitly by speaker and hearer, writer and reader, a *convention* which both observe. The poet should communicate with his readers in terms of contracts to which they are accustomed. If a reader knows a poem is to be an elegy or an epistle or a satire, then he is prepared to give it a certain kind of attention. Both the conventions of a particular genre and syntax itself are forms of contract which assist the poet to communicate with his reader. Words themselves are another type of contract, and, if civilised communication is to be achieved, it is essential that words should keep their relation to everyday meanings, and not be transformed into a private language by the poet himself.

Davie requires poets to mean what they say, and to relate their poems to common experience. His argument cannot be fully summarised here, and needs careful and detailed study. He is having a powerful effect on recent poetry and criticism, and on the way in which literary analysis is used today. His influence prevents a student from an endless search for new subtleties of interpretation, and sends him to study the nature of genres in particular periods. His emphasis on syntax, and the various types of syntax used by poets, offers new, exciting possibilities for analysis. He asserts the value of mind and rational order, and so offers tools with which a reader can assess the organisation of a long narrative poem. He tries to bring poetry back to traditional modes of communication, to make the poet, once again, a man speaking to men.

In *Romantic Image*, Frank Kermode follows Davie in attacking the view that the image is necessarily a superior mode of apprehension to conceptual thinking. He insists on the value of logical structures of thought, and points out that these are essential in Donne's technique. But Kermode's book is particularly famous for its attack on Eliot's dissociation theory. He shows that Hulme, Yeats and Eliot date this 'Fall' at different times, and that in fact the whole theory has no historical justification. The theory was produced by Eliot as an attempt to define what he himself was trying to achieve in verse; it should never have been used as an historical truth determining the way in which poems are analysed. Great poetry is not a mere series of reverberating images; it uses the machinery of ordinary discourse, and should offer readily available meanings to its readers. Art is made for men who habitually move in space and time, whose language is propelled onward by verbs, and the great tradition of verse is that which obeys conventional rules of meaning and syntax.

Many critics are also becoming conscious of certain moral dangers in the belief that 'there is a necessary relationship between the quality of the individual's response to art and his general fitness for a humane existence'. This view can easily lead to arrogance, and is of doubtful validity. Obviously the enjoyment of literature can give a person more tact and compassion, but we all know men of outstanding intelligence and sensitivity who are tone deaf to music, or wholly unable to enjoy poetry, drama, or the visual arts. And when this conception of the moral value of art is presented in its more extreme and fanatical forms, it leads to contempt for ordinary people, and to an overvaluing of a certain kind of intellectual élite. What would Dickens's Betsy Trotwood have made of a practical criticism test, one wonders, or his Joe Gargery? Yet of such, in life as in literature, is the Kingdom of Heaven.

4 Effects of these new ideas on practical analysis

Most of these objections are not directed towards practical criticism itself, but to its misuse. Most critics today do not wish to see the method abandoned, but would like it to be qualified in the light of experience. Practical criticism at its best ensures, for instance, that instead of repeating the opinions of his teachers, a student will have to make personal judgements of poems he has never seen before. He will have to look closely at the actual words being used, and describe precisely the effects of the poem. Although Helen Gardner's doubts should not be forgotten, teachers usually agree that they can help their students to pay attention to the true working of a poem, and so promote literary sensitivity.

The need today is for a proper teaching of practical criticism which avoids the obvious abuses of the method. One simple rule is that the poems analysed by a student should be worthy of admiration, and ones he might be expected to enjoy. There is no point in teaching a student that contemptuous tone of dismissal which has been one of the worst features of criticism during the last decades. Even the ordinary poems published week by week in *The Times Literary Supplement, The Observer* and *The Listener* are products of the creative mind, and superior to what most of us could achieve. Pleasure in minor verse is an essential part of the experience of reading, and no teacher of analysis should allow his students to feel in any way superior. Discrimination, the ability to differentiate between degrees of excellence, can be taught as part of appreciation, not depreciation. Many analysts in the past have spent too much time explaining what is wrong with a poem. This hypercritical attitude can do great damage both to reader and poet. A habit of superiority makes the reader lose his enjoyment of the variety of literary effects; it makes the poet himself self-conscious and timid in his use of words.

If a poem is bad this is usually obvious to anyone of reasonable sensitivity, and there is little point in pursuing it to its death. A useful analysis is almost always one which deals with a good poem (not necessarily a great one) and shows exactly why and how it is to be admired. Such appreciations avoid the pitfalls described by Helen Gardner and C. S. Lewis, and can assist a true development of sensibility. Eliot's theory of the unified sensibility implied that most poets are in some way lacking in fullness of life, and that by enjoying them the reader is indulging in inadequate satisfactions. This view led some critics to an excessive Puritanism, until a true sense of aesthetic values was almost lost. But poetry offers a variety of pleasures and a variety of gifts. By analysing the various ways in which the image has dominated recent thinking, Davie and Kermode have helped us to escape from the limitations of Eliot's theories.

How, then, should an analysis of a poem begin? The first question should always be: 'What kind of poem are we dealing with?' The answer to this question involves some discussion of the genre in which the poem is written, and the historical background. The tendency before 1950 was far too often to treat the poem as a self-sufficient unit, complete in itself and containing within its words all the material necessary for the analyst. But this view was very much influenced by the idea that the poem is an image, a unique reflection of reality embodied in a mode of communication which has always been available to poets. If, as Davie has argued, a poem is based upon a contract between writer and reader, an agreement about the conventions being employed, then knowledge of these conventions is the first prerequisite in understanding the poem. There is no point in offering an extract from Pope for analysis to someone who knows nothing of Pope's intentions and his methods of satire. The student, therefore, must have some knowledge of the author's life and times, and of the circumstances in which the poem was written. But he should not, of course, introduce into his analysis biographical or historical details that have no relevance to his elucidation of the poem.

Once the mode of communication has been established, the student should try to find some correspondence between the total effect of the poem on his sensibility and the actual words being used. If, after two or three readings, the poem has achieved no such effect, then there is little point in going on with the analysis. The student, in this case, needs to be taught more about the interactions of the words, in the hope that eventually he may perceive the literary effects. It is important that the student should want to analyse something to which his own sensibility has really responded. Only after such an experience will his analysis offer any sincere and valuable appreciation. There must be a real delight in the poem; otherwise practical criticism is certainly an academic exercise in the worst sense of that term.

The delight of the poem derives from its treatment of experience, and so the analysis should aim to deal precisely with the total meaning. When the aim, the genre and the background have been established, the student should consider the meaning, discussing the major themes and their development. But, in so doing, he should not offer a simple, cliché-ridden summary of attitudes to love or death or God; he should try to find words which do justice to the honest impression he himself has received. As he examines the poem, he should be able to think precisely about the effect of the meaning on himself, and this exact thinking should increase his appreciation of the poem's force or subtlety or profundity.

This analysis of themes should go side by side with an examination of technique. How does the total grammatical structure of the poem express the meaning? What is the effect of the arrangement of the lines? How does the poet use rhyme and rhythm? Is a traditional form being used such as the sonnet or blank verse, and if so, how does it relate to the history of poetic usage in these modes? What types of images are being employed, and how are they arranged? How are the ideas developed? What is the poet's tone of voice? How do the words build up that complex impression we received on first reading the poem?

And, finally, what has been achieved? Are there any weaknesses in the poem? Is the pleasure reduced by any lapses in technique? If we compare the poem with other ones of a similar kind, what degree of excellence is reached? All these questions are only pointers, for essentially practical criticism should be an experiment in reading, not the imposition of preconceived theories on a poem. The best practitioners submit themselves to the wide variety of literary effects, and are content to enjoy in a wise passiveness. Our own analyses obey no exercise-book rules, but try to record our liking for a representative group of twentieth-century poems.

5   Free verse

There is no space here to comment at length on the various verse forms used in the twentieth century, but perhaps a little should be said about free verse, the most distinctive new form of the age.

The concept of free verse is not unprecedented in English poetry, though its main inspiration was *vers libre* and came from France. Milton had used a form of free verse in *Samson Agonistes*, with results sometimes magnificent, sometimes rather wooden and dull; Coleridge's *Christabel* was a verse experiment moving towards a high degree of freedom. Not until the Imagists, however, did the form become widely used and discussed. The Imagists were in revolt against the type of poetry, very common towards the end of the nineteenth century, in which the content became the prisoner of the style. One thinks of precursors as early as Byron's

> The Assyrian came down like a wolf on the fold,
> And his cohorts were gleaming in purple and gold . . .

or Tennyson's

You must wake and call me early, call me early, mother dear;
Tomorrow'll be the happiest time of all the glad New-Year . . .

or Browning's

> I sprang to the stirrup, and Joris, and he;
> I galloped, Dirck galloped, we galloped all three . . .

Such poems may be very stirring and exciting to listen to, especially if they recognise their own limits and keep within them, but they cannot hope for very much in the way of variation or depth. The finished effect is liable to be emotionally as well as metrically jaunty. The Imagists rejected the whole principle on which such poems are built. They believed that each poem should start in an experience and seek for a style rather than the other way round. The style should be sufficiently flexible to develop with the meaning; the poem as a whole should be an individual experience (its music inseparable from the meaning, as T. S. Eliot was later to point out), and not just one more run through of an already hackneyed tune. In asking this, they were perhaps restating a condition necessary to all successful poetry, rather than propounding something strictly new. Even the great traditional forms, blank verse, heroic couplets, sonnets and so on, have, in the hands of major poets, taken on new and distinctive possibilities. In the writers of the past who inherited a style but pioneered in sensibility, creation has often amounted to a marriage between public style and private vision; the tension between these two has been a condition of creation. The Imagists, however, who inherited a situation where style seemed to have won a mastery over content, reacted towards the other extreme. The main experiment sanctioned and developed by the poets following them has been free verse; which is, as its name implies, the protest against a domination of meaning by style carried to its logical end. It was evolved in the belief that a poem's growth should be so conditioned by its theme that the rhythm will be at the service of tone and mood, and devices such as rhyme, assonance, regular metre and so on will be included or omitted, taken up or abandoned, just as the whole experience requires.

The rhythmic pattern will be unprescribed and unpredictable, and the poem will stop not according to rules, but when the logic of its own development is complete.

The three most celebrated exponents of free verse in the twenties all, however, differed greatly from one another in their handling of this form: T. S. Eliot, D. H. Lawrence and Ezra Pound. T. S. Eliot's verse, though free, is very far from being unattached to traditional disciplines. There is an underlying iambic norm in much of 'The Love Song of J. Alfred Prufrock', 'Portrait Of A Lady', 'Gerontion' and *The Waste Land* which creates the *feeling* of metrical pattern (as Graham Hough has pointed out in his chapter on free verse in *Image and Experience*, 1960) even though a counting of lines and syllables cannot always define this exactly. There is a unity of tone, and a patterning of theme and imagery which to some extent does the work traditionally assigned to rhyme and metre in directing the reading voice along meaningful paths. There are internal assonances and alliterations which one would not expect to find in prose. There is also a nearness of the speaking voice to ritual and incantation, a type of public voice which Eliot mastered very early in his career. This confers even on his early verse the suggestion of communal, and indeed religious significance; the very loneliness of Prufrock becomes a ritual, paradoxical though this may seem. The incantatory quality modifies strikingly the purely 'conversational' tone, which Eliot has always cultivated as a poet, and praised as a critic.

Other conventional affinities can also be traced. Eliot's early poems are often dramatic monologues influenced by both Browning and Jacobean Drama; their symbolism is avowedly indebted to Baudelaire and the French. *The Waste Land* itself is in a mock-heroic tradition that includes both Dryden and Pope among its ancestors. Eliot's frequent references to other literature, mostly through quotation or near quotation ironically intended, are integral to the structure; the verse itself makes a number of excursions into one conventional metre or another (these range from high tragedy, to snatches of a popular song) and the whole technique is obviously very different from prose. The structure of *Four Quartets*, written fifteen or so years later, is based on music, with interrelating themes and variations. This poem is possibly the culminating achievement of the freedom won from conventional verse forms, but in fulfilling free verse it also transmutes it into a new and highly subtle discipline of its own.

Of free verse as it was originally conceived, close to conversation and at times indistinguishable from prose, D. H. Lawrence is the earliest master. Poems like 'Snake' and 'The Ship of Death' demonstrate the great possibilities of this method whilst underlining, perhaps, the exceptional talent needed to carry it off. In throwing the poet back wholly upon personal experience, and almost wholly removing the tension between experience and literary form which has most usually been at the heart of poetic creation, it encourages him to rely to a dangerous extent on his own personality. The wrong *sort* of personal tone can easily usurp; one which ignores the poet's larger quest for universality in favour of the merely garrulous and gossipy. A similar flaw developed when certain poets of the later eighteenth century claimed the freedom to meditate in blank verse or rhyming couplets more or less as the fancy took them. If *The Task* is one example of the tediousness into which even a major poet can be lured by too great a technical freedom, the wreckage of Pound's *Cantos*—sometimes moving, often incomprehensible—is certainly another.

Perhaps it is with this in mind that many post-war poets have either abandoned free verse for strict metrical patterns (the Movement poets are an outstanding example of this), or have experimented with free verse of a more formal kind. Hopkins has had a considerable influence on Ted Hughes, and both R. S. Thomas and Thom Gunn have made interesting new experiments. These are discussed in detail in our analyses of

R. S. Thomas's 'A Blackbird Singing', Ted Hughes's 'The Casualty' and Thom Gunn's 'Considering the Snail'.

6 Characteristics of twentieth-century poetry

Our analyses chart the amazing developments of poetry that have taken place in this century. The poems of Edward Thomas and Walter de la Mare are representative of the best in the Georgian school, which dominated verse-writing round about the period of the Great War. This school treated personal themes in a romantic manner, and often used cliché-ridden imagery to describe the beauties of Nature, the delights of young love, or the quiet peace of old age. Owen and Lawrence transformed this style for their own unique purposes, but even their diction, particularly in early work, is Georgian in mood. It would be a mistake to generalise about Georgian poetry overmuch, as the recent Penguin Anthology has shown, but one can say that the poets called by this term, whatever their individual excellencies may have been, usually conformed to established rules of versification. With the exception of Owen and Lawrence they were not among the great innovators in our verse.

The great modern revolution in technique is best seen in the work of Eliot and Yeats. Revolutionary principles were offered by the Imagists, notably in their famous manifesto of 1913, but unhappily they included few poets of real merit. 'The Love Song of J. Alfred Prufrock' (published in 1917) and 'Easter 1916' (written in 1916, published in 1921) were among the earliest great poems in the new style. 'Easter 1916' showed that the dramatic development in Yeats's style, already familiar to readers of *The Wild Swans at Coole* (1919) was now complete: there was a new and vital urgency and concreteness, after the pleasant generalities of 'The Lake of Innisfree' and similar poems. 'Marina' is one of Eliot's mature poems, in which a sequence of images evokes precisely and with great beauty his developing religious attitudes.

The poets of the 1930's were specifically concerned with political themes. They were greatly influenced in their technique by Owen, Eliot and also Hopkins, whose poems were first published in 1918, nearly thirty years after his death. The most celebrated poets of this period, Auden, Spender, MacNeice and Day Lewis, were all very young men in their twenties, and their work has a youthful freshness and vigour. The two political poems represented here are Auden's 'Spain' (the most well known of all the poems about Spain) and Spender's 'The Landscape Near An Aerodrome'. C. Day Lewis is represented by a reflective poem, his sonnet sequence 'O Dreams, O Destinations', and Louis MacNeice by a lyric (a reminder, this, that this group of poets also wrote very fine lyrics, on all kinds of personal themes). There is also a poem by Michael Roberts, the most neglected poet of his time.

In the late 1930's and the 1940's the dominating voice was that of Dylan Thomas. Of all the poets since Eliot he is perhaps the most eccentric, but also the one of greatest genius. In many of his poems one feels that the language he uses is newly-minted: even clichés like 'To begin at the beginning' recapture their original excitement, almost miraculously, when he uses them. Dylan Thomas is represented here by 'Fern Hill', surely one of the most delightful poems of its time.

It was unfortunate, however, that Dylan Thomas's use of language was not of the kind to have a fruitful influence on poets of lesser gifts. He moved very far indeed from the normal structures of grammar and syntax and can be best discussed, perhaps, with Joyce, among our great but eccentric innovators in the use of words. An inevitable reaction against him occurred, and this was hastened by the emergence of a small, and inherently unimportant group of poets in the 1940's who called themselves the Apocalyptics. In the early 1950's the reaction against esoteric and experimental poetry became fully influential in the Movement, a group of poets including Philip Larkin and Thom Gunn whose anthology *New Lines*, published in 1957, restated some very traditional principles. Its editor, Robert Conquest, had this to say:

> It was in the late 1940's and early 1950's that a number of poets began to emerge who have been progressing from different viewpoints to a certain unity of approach, a new and healthy general standpoint.

> In one sense, indeed, the standpoint is not new, but merely the restoration of a sound and fruitful attitude to poetry, of the principle that poetry is written by and for the whole man, intellect, emotions, senses and all. But restorations are not repetitions. The atmosphere, the attack of these poets is as concentratedly contemporary as could be imagined. To be of one's own time is not an important virtue, but it is a necessary one.

> If one had briefly to distinguish this poetry of the fifties from its predecessors, I believe the most important general point would be that it submits to no great systems of theoretical constructs nor agglomerations of unconscious commands. It is free from both mystical and logical compulsions and—like modern philosophy—is empirical in its attitude to all that comes. This reverence for the real person or event is, indeed, a part of the general intellectual ambience (in so far as that is not blind or retrogressive) of our time. One might, without stretching matters too far, say that George Orwell with his principle of real, rather than ideological, honesty, exerted, even though indirectly, one of the major influences on modern poetry.

> On the more technical side, though of course related to all this, we see refusal to abandon a rational structure and comprehensible language, even when the verse is not highly charged with sensuous or emotional intent.

These theories are clearly akin to those of Donald Davie. They indicate why *The Waste Land* has had few imitators in recent years, and why Dylan Thomas's reputation has suffered a temporary eclipse. In *Image and Experience*, Graham Hough has argued that the post-1950 verse is a return to the proper tradition of poetry. The 'modern' movement produced much great verse, but was moving down a road with a dead-end. In the twentieth century, the true tradition is represented by Hardy, Graves, Edwin Muir, Larkin, even Betjeman. The images used by these poets may be richly significant, but at the same time their poems offer a straightforward, rational meaning. The poet no longer sees himself as an alien speaking in a special language to a few initiates. He feels himself, as the great Romantics did, as a man speaking to men in a suffering world.

Why has this major change occurred since 1950 in both verse and criticism? The Cambridge school represented by Graham Hough, Donald Davie and John Holloway has had much to do with it, but no single answer could be satisfactory. Two of the best poets since the war are Ted Hughes and R. S. Thomas, both of whom have been little influenced by any of the trends we have touched on here, yet they, too, unmistakably belong to our time.

The Waste Land, the *Cantos* and much of the poetry between the wars recorded the chaos of the post-1918 world. Since 1950 we live in an even more dangerous world, threatened by nuclear bombs, but the direct impact of this upon poetry is very much less. Perhaps to detect it we have to look slightly below the surface. Ted Hughes suggests the violence of modern society in his images of animal life and pre-atomic warfare, Thom Gunn in his complex and sympathetic response to the teddy boys and ton-up boys of our age. But both of these poets refuse to fall into despair, and in this they are characteristic of the new trend. Philip Larkin proves that order can be created in small areas of personal relationships; R. S. Thomas continues to find real and deep meanings in the life of simple men close to the soil. The new poets express much compassion for the ordinary human condition, and through their art demonstrate that the mind can still impose some order on the chaotic experience of twentieth-century living. To ask why poetry has turned in this direction is to seek an understanding of the whole temper of the mind of Britain today. The poetry of the 1960's expresses our own moods and fears. We hope that our analyses of modern poems will persuade readers to look with pleasure and profit at the large number of good and sometimes great poems being written today.

I

AFTER A JOURNEY *by Thomas Hardy*

HERETO I come to view a voiceless ghost;
　　Whither, O whither will its whim now draw me?
Up the cliff, down, till I'm lonely, lost,
　　And the unseen waters' ejaculations awe me.
Where you will next be there's no knowing,
　　Facing round about me everywhere,
　　　　With your nut-coloured hair,
And gray eyes, and rose-flush coming and going.

Yes: I have re-entered your olden haunts at last;
　　Through the years, through the dead scenes I have tracked
　　　　you;
What have you now found to say of our past—
　　Scanned across the dark space wherein I have lacked you?
Summer gave us sweets, but autumn wrought division?
　　Things were not lastly as firstly well
　　　　With us twain, you tell?
But all's closed now, despite Time's derision.

I see what you are doing: you are leading me on
　　To the spots we knew when we haunted here together,
The waterfall, above which the mist-bow shone
　　At the then fair hour in the then fair weather,
And the cave just under, with a voice still so hollow
　　That it seems to call out to me from forty years ago,
　　　　When you were all aglow,
And not the thin ghost that I now frailly follow!

Ignorant of what there is flitting here to see,
  The waked birds preen and the seals flop lazily;
Soon you will have, Dear, to vanish from me,
  For the stars close their shutters and the dawn whitens hazily.
Trust me, I mind not, though Life lours,
  The bringing me here; nay, bring me here again!
    I am just the same as when
Our days were a joy, and our paths through flowers.

Hardy's first wife, Emma, died in November, 1912. After her death, he discovered that she had written three very personal manuscripts about her life. The first two were so distressing to him that he destroyed them. The third, *Some Recollections*,[1] includes reminiscences about Emma's early life. An account of her happy childhood is followed by an enthusiastic description of her first meetings with Hardy. On reading the manuscript Hardy was stricken with remorse, for their later married life had been extremely unhappy. In the early months of 1913, he revisited the places in Cornwall, where their young love had flourished, and 'After a Journey' describes this search into the past. Some of his best poems were written at this time. He composed at least fifty poems concerning Emma during the year after her death, and many of these recall phrases or incidents from *Some Recollections*. She tells how she showed Hardy 'the solemn small shores where the seals lived, coming out of great caverns very occasionally', and this detail Hardy uses in his poem.

'After a Journey' is a most suitable poem with which to introduce a study of twentieth-century verse. Both its mood of uncertainty and its personal rhythms point forward to characteristically modern developments. Hardy published his last novel, *Jude the Obscure*, in 1895, and from this time until his death in

---

[1] Emma Hardy, *Some Recollections*, edited by Evelyn Hardy and Robert Gittings; together with some relevant poems by Thomas Hardy. Oxford University Press, 1961.

1928 devoted himself to poetry. Jude has much in common with the heroes of many twentieth-century novels. He does not have deep roots in his community, but becomes homeless, moving from place to place in search of a fulfilment he cannot find. There is a strong element of autobiography in Hardy's depiction of Jude, and the perplexities dramatised in this novel become the theme of his later verse. On a first reading a poem such as 'After a Journey' might seem a conventional piece of nostalgic writing, but its surface simplicity covers a profound, almost tragic awareness of the enigma of human life. As in Walter de la Mare's 'The Listeners' and Edward Thomas's 'The Sign-Post', with which we deal next, the apparent conventionality of theme and treatment hides highly original attitudes of mind. These poets do not employ the experimental techniques of Ezra Pound and T. S. Eliot, but they are similarly oppressed by the loneliness of modern man. They are still using typical romantic language and imagery, but these are transformed by the pressure of personal experience.

Hardy was a young man when in 1859 Darwin's *Origin of Species* was published. The theory of evolution persuaded some writers, such as G. B. Shaw, to believe that civilisation was developing new and better forms, and that we were moving towards a society of supermen. In contrast, Hardy was disturbed by the breakdown of traditional Christian beliefs, and became increasingly pessimistic. He tried to find some rational explanation for the mystery of the universe, but his doubts grew like a cloud over his sensibility. 'After a Journey', like so many of the later poems, considers death with a most disturbing honesty, and offers few consolations. T. S. Eliot and W. B. Yeats succeeded in some degree in reconciling religion with rationalism. Eliot became a Christian and Yeats developed his own individual brand of mysticism. Their verse is not without doubts and equivocations, but in many great poems they escape from pessimism. Hardy, De la Mare and Edward Thomas are typically modern in their acceptance of uncertainty, and this is one reason why they have had so much influence on post-1950 verse.

Recent poets have been influenced not only by Hardy's personal self-questionings, but also by his technique as a poet. Just as the traditional, countryside way of life, celebrated in early novels such as *Under the Greenwood Tree*, breaks down, and characters such as Clym Yeobright, Tess and Jude become isolated, so Hardy's poetic language moves from simple, musical ballads to the individual tone of voice in 'After a Journey'. The importance of Hardy in the development of modern verse has often been underestimated. When the *Collected Poems* were published, Ezra Pound wrote: 'Now *there* is a clarity. There *is* the harvest of having written 20 novels first.' W. H. Auden, Dylan Thomas and Philip Larkin have all testified to their debt to Hardy. Like Browning, whom he studied with admiration, Hardy escapes from the conventional rhythms of Swinburne towards a more conversational, dramatic manner. The voice that speaks in 'After a Journey' is quiet, gentle, melancholy and completely honest. There are no false postures, or bardic pretence, only an uncompromising reflection of deeply moving personal experience. It is this honesty which has particularly influenced Larkin, and poems of his such as 'No Road' and 'Church Going' owe much to Hardy.

The construction of 'After a Journey' provides a good example of Hardy's mature technique. The rhyme scheme—ab ab cd dc —is regular in each stanza, and contributes much to the lyrical quality of the poem. The short, penultimate line, rhyming with the previous one, assists this singing quality of the verse. We are reminded of Hardy's love of music, and that he spent much time in studying metrical forms and in trying to achieve novel sound effects. Lines such as 'Summer gave us sweets, but autumn wrought division' and 'For the stars close their shutters and the dawn whitens hazily' have a rich and poignant music. But this lyrical quality is repeatedly disturbed and broken in the poem, and this innovation points forward to the later development of free verse. The first line of the poem—'Hereto I come to view a voiceless ghost'—has five clear, stresses, and is a normal iambic line; but the second line, personal and questioning, immediately breaks down this regular pattern. The alliteration in 'whither' and 'whim' continues the lyrical effect, but the rhythm is close now to the speaking voice. The words 'will', 'whim', 'now', 'draw', and 'me' are all stressed in some degree. 'Whim' is heavily stressed, and then the last three words have a slow movement, as if Hardy is pondering over this question. In the third line, the movement reflects the experience precisely, and there is no attempt to impose an iambic pattern. The long pauses after 'cliff', 'down', 'lonely' and 'lost' suggest both the uncertain moments of the narrator, following this spirit of his wife, and his emotional condition, not knowing any longer how to move purposefully in this world. The fourth line is typical in its mixture of a lyrical tone with the personal speaking voice. Like nearly all the rhymes in the poem, 'awe me' is a full rhyme, adding to the sense of pattern and musical effect. A break in the movement of the line is made by the two unstressed syllables that lie together at the end of 'waters' and 'ejaculations'. This break in the lyrical flow suggests Hardy's own voice; but the music of this line, one of the most evocative in the poem, is almost beyond analysis. This mixture of lyricism and conversational tone continues throughout the poem. There are many feminine endings to lines—'draw me', 'awe me', 'knowing', 'going', 'tracked you', 'lacked you', etc.—and these, making the lines drop away at the end, create the prevailing melancholy cadences of the poem. Although the rhyme scheme is constant from stanza to stanza, and the penultimate line is always short, the number of syllables in each line conform to no fixed pattern. The fifth line, for example, has nine syllables in the first stanza, twelve in the second, thirteen in the third, and eight in the fourth. The arrangement of stresses and syllables accords with the demands of

Hardy's experience, and works in opposition to any conventional metrics.

In all his poems Hardy continues to introduce 'poeticism'. There are many words and phrases taken straight from romantic jargon—'Whither, O whither', 'olden haunts', 'wrought' 'twain', and 'Life lours'—in 'After a Journey'. These archaic words might suggest at a first quick glance that the poem is simple and traditional, recording a universal experience of loss. But the accuracy of the observations, both of the scene itself and of personal emotions, makes this use of language by no means conventional. We see how 'the waked birds preen and the seals flop lazily', and we are given a most poignant description of Hardy's own feelings. As in the poetry of de la Mare and Edward Thomas, old poeticisms are given a new flavour.

Lyricism and the speaking voice, poeticisms and precise descriptions, combine to present Hardy's dramatic sense of the influence of the past on the present. The poem shifts between the pictures of young love and the situation of the old man, wandering just before dawn through these old familiar scenes. As always in Hardy, the contrast is between a simple, happy past and an uncertain present. Although the poem describes a moment in time, when the poet's memories of his wife are so acute that he feels her presence like a ghost, the moment achieves its rich significance because of its relation to the past. The poem shifts backwards and forwards between past and present, until we hardly know in what period of time we are living. The feeling of transience is overwhelming. As Hardy revisits the cliff, the waterfall and the cave, his experience is almost like a dream, an illusion of the senses. We feel the contrast between his present wanderings and the warm-blooded reality of the past, between the wraith-like spirit who leads him on and the young girl, with her nut-coloured hair, grey eyes and rose-flushed cheeks.

From the beginning the poem is full of uncertainty. The ghost is voiceless, unable to ascribe any meaning to death, drawing

Hardy back into the past. The 'unseen waters' evoke a sense of great beauty, but also suggest danger. It is night, and the noise of the sea is like some voice from the other side of life, speaking to him through the darkness of the mind. In the second stanza Hardy recalls the failure of his marriage. Through 'the dead scenes', 'the dark space', he tries to find again the young girl he once loved. With an unequivocal sincerity he writes: 'Things were not lastly as firstly well With us twain . . .' The archaic language makes this simple acknowledgement of failure profoundly moving. The third stanza begins with Hardy speaking intimately to his dead wife. Their melancholy tone, followed by pictures from the past, remind us of the pathos of the fading of love. The fact that Emma Hardy is dead obtrudes through all the fancies of the poem. The intimate tone is directed to a person who exists in the past, and who can never be recalled. This indicates the correct interpretation of the last stanza. Dawn approaches, and the birds and seals move about with no thought for the past. As in traditional stories, the ghost must disappear at cock-crow. The tender word 'Dear', followed by 'vanish', reminds us that these memories, so powerful at this moment, must also fade. These lines not only reflect Hardy's own loss, but link his grief with the dying faiths of his time. The old romantic certainties, with their glorification of man, have no meaning in the twentieth century. The image of the stars closing their shutters reminds us of much other modern literature, picturing the dying of the light and the birth of despair. Hardy is particularly successful in his poetry in evoking a sense of twilight or gloom. The 'unseen waters', the stars closing 'their shutters', the dawn whitening 'hazily', beautifully suggest the half-light through which he moves.

After these uncertainties and the overwhelming nostalgia for the past, the last three lines become a pitiful cry. He is not the same as forty years ago. The time when 'our days were a joy, and our paths through flowers' is gone for ever. Yet 'despair' is not quite the right word with which to end this study of 'After a Journey'. Hardy concludes the poem by asking to be brought again to such moments when his mind is invaded by the wonder of the past; and there is a quality of stoic acceptance in the honest recognition of the facts of his experience. His journey brings him to the half-light of an incomprehensible world. He rejects all comfortable belief in progress, and shoulders the burden of the twentieth-century consciousness.

2

THE LISTENERS *by Walter de la Mare*

'Is there anybody there?' said the Traveller,
  Knocking on the moonlit door;
And his horse in the silence champed the grasses
  Of the forest's ferny floor:
And a bird flew up out of the turret,
  Above the Traveller's head:
And he smote upon the door again a second time;
  'Is there anybody there?' he said.
But no one descended to the Traveller;
  No head from the leaf-fringed sill
Leaned over and looked into his grey eyes,
  Where he stood perplexed and still.
But only a host of phantom listeners
  That dwelt in the lone house then
Stood listening in the quiet of the moonlight
  To that voice from the world of men:
Stood thronging the faint moonbeams on the dark stair,
  That goes down to the empty hall,
Hearkening in an air stirred and shaken
  By the lonely Traveller's call.
And he felt in his heart their strangeness,
  Their stillness answering his cry,
While his horse moved, cropping the dark turf
  'Neath the starred and leafy sky;

For he suddenly smote on the door, even
   Louder, and lifted his head:—
'Tell them I came, and no one answered,
   That I kept my word', he said.
Never the least stir made the listeners,
   Though every word he spake
Fell echoing through the shadowiness of the still house
   From the one man left awake:
Ay, they heard his foot upon the stirrup,
   And the sound of iron on stone,
And how the silence surged softly backward,
   When the plunging hoofs were gone.

'The Listeners' is about silence and loneliness, as de la Mare's poems usually are. Even the title makes clear that the Traveller, though his is the only human voice in the poem, matters less than the listeners, who say nothing, are phantoms, and can hardly be separated from the silence surrounding them. Into the silence and solitude, again typically, there rides a single man. De la Mare's world is a world of one; there are no relationships in it, either to people, or to places, or to time. The Traveller might be Any Man, the episode Any Time and Any Place, as in a sense they are.

One begins with the tone and mood: dreamlike, in that the scene is unlocalised, yet remarkably clear and precise too in the details, as dreams often are. The moonlight is the moonlight of all romantic poetry, a setting for experience heightened beyond the common-place towards what might be insight, might be hallucination. To the poet himself it seems real enough, and he turns it into words that fascinate readers of all ages, whether they 'understand' what is being said or not. The horse, the bird, the forest, the turret, the leaf-fringed sill are fixed in a moment of intense expectation, against the moonlight and the enfolding silence. They help like the words of the Traveller himself, to define the silence. His question 'Is there anybody there?', his last challenge 'Tell them I came, and no one answered' resonate against the silence, underlining its enigma and its finality. The poem is called 'The Listeners', but any listeners there might be do not declare themselves.

In all of de la Mare's poems, humanity is stripped of social and historical context. His people are shadowy; we have no way of knowing anything about them, except that they are very old, very beautiful, very gay, very sad. When they turn into ghosts, as they sometimes do (the exquisite 'Three Cherry Trees' is an excellent example), they seem scarcely altered. The landscape alters round them; the silence steals gradually closer, as it does in this poem, waiting until they have finished and it is left in total possession again. They have no class, no period, no *Zeit-geist*, no personal history. You can push them back indefinitely into the world of the dead, 'Twenty, forty, sixty, eighty, A hundred years ago' . . . but they are still in no historical past. Their one major relationship, as the absence of particular relationships serves to underline, is with transience; their isolation is that of the soul itself, inside the laws of change. If they live anywhere, it is in the world of the family album, and the strangely timeless reality and unreality of that. Their gaiety, beauty, sadness, just because they have no immediate context, directly confront the certainty of decay.

Loneliness is, as we all know, one of the frequent themes of twentieth-century writers. Usually it has a social setting—it is the loneliness of the saint or the sinner, the king or the beggar, the genius or the half-wit, the hero or the coward, the betrayed or the betrayer, or what you will. All of these lonelinesses are defined against, and relate to, something. Normally the writer approves or disapproves, sometimes he has suggestions or a programme; he may feel that life is tragic in itself. In de la Mare, loneliness is defined against nothing: indeed, it relates to the perennial human awareness of nothing, which underlies our particular histories, often tinging them with a sense of the unreal. To be obsessed with this awareness, as de la Mare was, is admittedly morbid, yet undeniably it is part of our human predicament, as poems such as the one we are considering remind us. The loneliness of the soul in itself, somewhere between waking and sleeping, between midnight and dawn. This is de la Mare's territory, and inside it there are few to equal him.

The time and the place are unspecific: why, then, is everything so vivid? Why does this particular poem, like many others by de la Mare, haunt the mind?—really haunt it, with a resolute resistance to exorcism? Partly, perhaps, because the very remoteness of the Traveller and his situation from historical particulars sets them free as symbols. The whole poem is like a dream, which may be diversely and plausibly interpreted after we wake, but which has its own symbolic vividness beyond any or all of the meanings it can be shown to have. In 'The Listeners', the human protagonist is the Traveller, who has journeyed to this moonlit door to keep faith with whoever he expects to find there. We have no idea where he comes from or where he rides off to at the end. All we are told about him is that he comes on a horse, that his eyes are grey, and that he is the one man left awake. We know nothing of the purpose of his journey except that the other side does not seem to have kept faith. Is he a sane man lost in a world of illusions? He might be. What we do know is that his parting words have a finality, heroic yet forlorn, which resonates against the other finality of the silence, and lingers with it in unresolved enigma as the poem passes into our memory:

> 'Tell them I came, and no one answered,
>   That I kept my word', he said.

The situation, and the poem, do not derive from any other literary source; they neither copy nor evoke anything that has been written before. Inevitably, however, one is reminded of various quests in writers of the past, and of other richly symbolic landscapes in European literature. A quest; a lonely yet undefeated traveller; a strange landscape, pregnant with evocations yet eluding exact analysis; a moment of arrival which vibrates with significance, yet to which no definitive meaning can be attached. As symbolism, the setting has all the material for an exploration of the meaning of existence itself. 'Is there anybody there?'—most of us have asked the Traveller's question at some time, with ears strained for some answering sound from the listeners. And the quest itself is familiar, guided by loyalties which might or might not be honoured, to ends not always known. The very absence of information about the 'them' this particular Traveller has come to meet enables us to feel all the more the relevance to our own dark future meetings. And one notices, as has already been implied, that the fact of the Traveller on his side keeping faith is connected with the serenity of the poem's tone; it is important in itself, whether he gets an answer or not. What de la Mare does is to dramatise, with exquisite precision, the moment of challenge and doubt when the isolated soul questions the unanswering universe. He does more. He dramatises, at the same time, the silence and the enigma of the listeners; the meeting of a human with the great and strange silence, in a moment that is not without dignity.

To this silence the poem always returns. It is so tangible, you can almost touch it. Nothingness itself comes near to incarnation:

> But no one descended to the Traveller;
> No head from the leaf-fringed sill
> Leaned over and looked into his grey eyes
> Where he stood perplexed and still.

No one descends; no head leans over and looks: it is the nearest approach to meeting no one that we are likely to make. And the listeners themselves, who walk off with the title of the poem, make no stir, but *are* the silence they lurk in, just as the witches in *Macbeth* are the air into which they vanish. At the end, the silence 'surges softly backwards', and remains when the plunging hoofs are gone.

Why is it all so vivid, despite the shadowiness of time and place? I have suggested the symbolic richness as one explanation. Another is to be found in the language of the poem, which is almost paradoxically concrete and clear. Throughout his poems, de la Mare makes frequent use, as he does here, of words like 'lone', 'empty', 'phantom', 'strangeness'. These words we tend to associate with the Georgian poets, whose lavish use debases them to routine gestures, making the evocation inherent in the words themselves do work that should be done by the poet. De la Mare escapes this general criticism. He reminds us that these words, like any other, have a 'central' usage, abused as they might be as poetic clichés. Reading 'The Listeners', we sense the eerie quality in the situation as a whole; the numinous words belong to, rather than create, the atmosphere. Far from leaning on our own sense of the strange for his effect, de la Mare actually extends and deepens it in his verse. His odd, but impressive achievement has been to make the strange, the non-existent even, almost tangible, with the tangibility that language and poetry can confer. The whole effect is paradoxical and unusual; one does not wish other poets to imitate it, and is not surprised if they debase the effect when they do. But it is, in its own right, an important awareness—at the very end of one of the roads of romanticism, if one thinks in literary terms; but also a possibility permanently underlying most human experience. If we decide that it is a cul-de-sac in the maze of life, at least it is one that most of us wander into at times; especially when we doubt whether there really is a centre to find.

There is one final thing to draw attention to: the childlike quality in Walter de la Mare's best work. Although he brings us to the brink of dereliction, he never topples us over. Something of the freshness of childish fantasy, a hint of magic, is always there as well. The child's never-never land, where all dreams might be realised and all 'ifs' might come true, is not too far away. It is no accident that de la Mare should also be our greatest modern writer of children's verse, and that his best verse for children should be as good as his best poetry for adults—almost indistinguishable from it, in fact.

The magic never actually happens. The 'ifs' go on sounding, with unquenchable freshness, but is there anyone there, listening? The poem we have been considering is what de la Mare has to say about that.

3

THE SIGN-POST *by Edward Thomas*

THE dim sea glints chill. The white sun is shy,
And the skeleton weeds and the never-dry,
Rough, long grasses keep white with frost
At the hilltop by the finger-post;
The smoke of the traveller's-joy is puffed
Over hawthorn berry and hazel tuft.
I read the sign. Which way shall I go?
A voice says: You would not have doubted so
At twenty. Another voice gentle with scorn
Says: At twenty you wished you had never been born.

One hazel lost a leaf of gold
From a tuft at the tip, when the first voice told
The other he wished to know what 'twould be
To be sixty by this same post. 'You shall see,'
He laughed—and I had to join his laughter—
'You shall see; but either before or after,
Whatever happens, it must befall,
A mouthful of earth to remedy all
Regrets and wishes shall freely be given;
And if there be a flaw in that heaven
'Twill be freedom to wish, and your wish may be
To be here or anywhere talking to me,
No matter what the weather, on earth,
At any age between death and birth,—
To see what day or night can be,
The sun and the frost, the land and the sea,

Summer, Autumn, Winter, Spring,—
With a poor man of any sort, down to a king,
Standing upright out in the air
Wondering where he shall journey, O where?'

Edward Thomas is best known for anthology pieces such as
'Adlestrop' and 'Tall Nettles'. These poems record his lyrical
delight at the beauty of the English countryside:

And for that minute a blackbird sang
Close by, and round him, mistier,
Farther and farther, all the birds
Of Oxfordshire and Gloucestershire.

Such poems are similar to the conventional descriptive verse of
the Georgian period, but are given freshness by his accurate
observations and by a certain originality in his attitudes. There
are moments when Thomas is not in the least like the usual
Georgian Nature poet, and when he appears to be putting
forward some very odd and disturbing viewpoints.

In 'The Sign-Post', these unusual attitudes are more explicit
than elsewhere, and this makes the poem highly original. The
opening description is a typical Georgian device, setting the
atmosphere for the reflections that are to follow; but this landscape is very different from the calm twilights and moonlit
vistas of the poetasters of the time. The assonance in 'dim',
'glints' and 'chill' gives these words extra stress, making the sea
appear cold and forbidding. The words 'white' and 'shy' not
only provide a striking picture of a sun not powerful enough to
thaw the frost, but also suggest a certain neutrality in the scene.
The sea is 'dim', and the sun 'shy', as if all vitality has been withdrawn. The sun will not interfere, to impose bold lines of shadow
and light on this landscape. The skeleton weeds and the rough,
long grasses are not symbols of Nature's abundance, but
suggest a world where life exists with difficulty. The setting is

appropriate to a poem that is to be about the impossibility
of ever knowing with certainty where we are going, or why.

The words spoken by the second voice are surprising, and it is
possible to read this poem a number of times without being sure
of Thomas's intentions. The poem has a curious backward
movement. The first voice criticises the poet for his uncertainty;
but we are not allowed to remain fixed in this new viewpoint.
Immediately the second voice scornfully rejects the illusion that
the poet had any more certainty when he was twenty, or that he
will have when he is sixty. The only certainty is death, when a
mouthful of earth will provide a free remedy for all regrets and
wishes. But the thought of the poem does not stay here, but
moves backward again. The second voice puts forward the very
unusual idea that oblivion would be a heaven, but that death
itself may have a flaw, that you will be free to wish, and that
your wish may be to return to life and its condition of uncertainty. And so the argument moves backwards to end where it
began, with a man looking at a sign-post, and wondering which
way to go.

The second voice speaks in a most delightful ironic tone. At
times the irony is playful, as when he laughs at the inevitability
of old age, or hints that the poet would prefer to be back talking
'with a poor man of any sort, down to a king'. But the irony is
also more serious, putting forward that balance or tension of
opposites which represents Thomas's total conception of life.
The poem expresses a deep longing to escape from the burden
of existence. 'At twenty you wished you had never been born',
the second voice tells him, and 'A mouthful of earth' would be
'heaven'. But this pessimism is balanced by a powerful response
to the pleasures of living. Even in the opening lines, the neutral
landscape is not without beauty, and the flowers of traveller's
joy and the gold leaf of the hazel are recorded with pleasure.
After the references to death, the poem suddenly breaks into a
lyric cry of delight at the glory of the world, of day and night,

land and sea, summer, autumn, winter, spring. There is an all-inclusiveness about these lines, a tone of celebration in complete contrast to the words of the tired traveller, uncertain which way to go. The irony maintains a balance between these two attitudes, and neither predominates. After the lyrical outburst, and the fine, dignified picture of the human race 'standing upright out in the air', the ironic last line reminds us that to participate in this joy is to be back asking questions, not knowing what to make of one's life. The total meaning of the poem is an ironic comment on man's predicament. We are always wanting to go somewhere, to make something different of our lives. Yet to live, to be part of the human race, with its joys and uncertainties, we must remain at the sign-post. Just as the poem moves backwards, unable to accept any definitive view of life, so human experience cannot escape from doubt. The acceptance of this condition is perhaps the true way of life, and the only possible freedom.

These balancing attitudes are mimed by Thomas's use of rhythm and rhyme. Much of the poem is in the Georgian mode. It is written in couplets, and at times, particularly in the concluding lines, there are pronounced lyrical rhythms. We feel that Thomas thinks of the poet as a man who creates beauty. But he also allows himself much freedom in his line arrangement and rhythms. Lines vary between seven and twelve syllables. Some lines such as 'To see what day or night can be', have a firm iambic beat, while many others are very close to the emphases of the speaking voice. The lyrical conclusion becomes more striking because it emerges out of the conversational, ironic rhythms. Just as the poem expresses uncertainty in its thought, so the tone shifts from one style to the other. In Thomas's best poems, all written in a short period before he was killed in 1917, he escapes from the conventional iambic beat, and creates a distinctive, personal tone of voice. In 'The Sign-Post', the alternation between lyricism and irony provides a striking medium for the tension in himself between joy and doubt.

4

FUTILITY *by Wilfred Owen*

Move him into the sun—
Gently its touch awoke him once,
At home, whispering of fields unsown.
Always it woke him, even in France,
Until this morning and this snow.
If anything might rouse him now
The kind old sun will know.

Think how it wakes the seeds,—
Woke, once, the clays of a cold star.
Are limbs, so dear-achieved, are sides,
Full-nerved—still warm—too hard to stir?
Was it for this the clay grew tall?
—O what made fatuous sunbeams toil
To break earth's sleep at all?

Wilfred Owen's poem is a memorial to an Unknown Soldier; a poetic equivalent, in its way, to the famous Tomb in Westminster Abbey. We have no idea who the dead man is; we do not know whether he was even known to the poet, except in his death. Like the Unknown Soldier he is nameless, but with an anonymity at the opposite pole to abstraction. Our most personal experiences of love and loss respond for him. He is every young man dead and squandered in war.

The economy of the poem is remarkable. It is short enough to be inscribed on a tomb, and has something of the same finality.

The vocabulary is simple and homely. Nearly all the words are monosyllabic: they move with an even tread, until the second stanza, lines three to four, when this evenness is deliberately broken, to point the mounting emotional intensity. Notice the very characteristic use of assonance—sun/sown; once/France; snow/now/know; seeds/sides; star/stir; tall/toil/all. These half-rhymes leave a sense of incompleteness on the ear. Cheated of our natural expectation of a rhyme, we are referred back from the poem itself as a formal triumph (which it is) to the poem's theme: to the frustration of form, of pattern, in the ruthless destructiveness of war.

The poem's tone is governed by the imperatives and questions through which it progresses. All of these are tinged with irony, of the kind peculiar to imperatives when there is nothing useful to be done, and to questions when there is nothing hopeful to be known. The words introducing these imperatives and questions are 'Move' (line 1), 'If' (line 6), 'Think' (line 8), 'Are' (line 10), 'Was it' (line 12) and 'O what' (line 13).

The word 'move' is not a literal imperative, since Owen is not addressing anyone on the spot. The dead man is not really to be moved into the sun, and we know that it could no longer reach him if he were. The imperative is, therefore, profoundly ironic, though its main function is of another kind. The real directive is to the reader; we are mentally to move the dead body into contrast with the life-giving sun—a contrast which is to permeate the poem as a whole. The force of this is nearer to contemplation than to action, nearer to a question than to a normal imperative. 'Futility' is, indeed, a passionate meditation, conducted by the poet in the presence of any of us who choose to hear.

In line 2 the word 'gently' intensifies the ironic suggestiveness established in the first line, of loving care in a situation where love and care are no longer of any use. Gentleness is linked with the sun, which takes on attributes first of parental love (the 'kind old

53

sun' waking a young man in the mornings of life), and then of godhead:

> Think how it woke the seeds,—
> Woke, once, the clays of a cold star . . .

The sun is certainly a symbol of life, and may even in the chemistry of creation have been its cause, but all the suggestions surrounding it are ironic. The word 'awoke' reminds us of our own summer wakings to a world of promise and hope, but the very reminder is through a desolating realisation that for this man, in this place, waking and hoping already belong to the past. The 'always' in line 4 is in fact an 'always until', though the word 'until' is held back until line 5 where it comes, after dominating line 4 by its unstated presence, with tremendous effect. The phrase 'fields unsown' simultaneously evokes the rich promises of youth, with all of life stretching out before, and the bitter certainty that these particular fields never will be sown: even in presenting itself, the promise is conjured from the future into the past. Then in line 6 we pass to a rhetorical condition:

> If anything might rouse him now
> The kind old sun will know.

There is no real 'if' here, as we very well know. This is that agonising 'if', more poignant perhaps than any word in the language, with which we ponder something that might once have been alterable, but is now fixed and terrible in the past. It directs our attention even more harrowingly to the sun, in its enigmatic relationship with the dead man. Why should this life-giving warmth, which brought him gently and patiently to life, be so utterly helpless at the very moment of death? The poem actually challenges sentimentality, in the phrase 'the kind old sun'—only, however, to confront it with an annihilating bitterness: with the certainty that since the 'if' is not real, then to weep, or to scold, or to appeal will be equally without avail.

The sun is confronted with the final coldness beyond its powers. The implications of the opening line are realised in the fullest degree.

Stanza 2 opens with another imperative, even further removed from action than the first. 'Think how it wakes the seeds . . .' As the poet moves to a wider questioning of creation itself, he also deepens our sense of the personal. The soldier does not simply represent mystery, he *is* the mystery incarnate. The poem proceeds to its central questions, impassioned and resonant, which carry what has gone before to a new level of agonised clarity:

> Are limbs so dear-achieved, are sides
> Full-nerved—still warm—so hard to stir?

That 'still warm', referring back as it does to the sun, is almost unbearable. Only after this does the anger underlying the question become fully explicit—in the final question, charged with its own bitter answer:

> O what made fatuous sunbeams toil
> To break earth's sleep at all?

Why did all this suffering have to be? It is the cry of Job.

What, we may ask in conclusion, is the poem's theme? The obvious answer can be given in Owen's own famous words, 'war, and the pity of war'. (It is interesting to compare 'Futility' with other attitudes to violent death that can be found in this collection: with Yeats's 'Easter 1916', Auden's 'Spain', and Ted Hughes's 'The Casualty'.) Behind the poem's very existence there is protest at the folly of men, who have turned creation into destruction, and effected this terrible despoiling of youth.

But notice that though the protest is certainly savage, it is never cynical. Owen's close attention to the dead man is inseparable from human compassion. He believes that an individual still matters, and not least in the moment of his death. The poem's title is 'Futility', but deeper levels of futility have been plumbed since he wrote. The mass slaughter of the mid-twentieth century has led some writers to doubt whether individuals have any meaning or value at all. Wilfred Owen is well on the other side, the human side, of *that* futility. His lament for a unique individual is closer to tragedy than to despair.

And this suggests a final comment, which must surely be made. Though the poem's theme is war, it is also a poem about death. Is it not profoundly relevant to any death, and to any premature death especially, whether in battle or not? In its deepest implications 'Futility' is not only a social protest but a religious questioning. It faces the mystery of life in sentiments that would remain profoundly true for the bereaved, even if war itself could by some miracle be abolished. The 'futility' of the title does not refer simply to human follies; it refers beyond these, also, to the human condition itself. It is one side of the tragic vision of man—the perception that if man is the jest and riddle of the world, this is only because he is first and chiefly its glory. The poem moves through questions which are essentially religious, whether they are accompanied by religious belief or not.

5

EASTER 1916 *by W. B. Yeats*

I HAVE met them at close of day
Coming with vivid faces
From counter or desk among grey
Eighteenth-century houses.
I have passed with a nod of the head
Or polite meaningless words,
Or have lingered awhile and said
Polite meaningless words,
And thought before I had done
Of a mocking tale or a gibe
To please a companion
Around the fire at the club,
Being certain that they and I
But lived where motley is worn:
All changed, changed utterly:
A terrible beauty is born.

That woman's days were spent
In ignorant good-will,
Her nights in argument
Until her voice grew shrill.
What voice more sweet than hers
When, young and beautiful,
She rode to harriers?
This man had kept a school
And rode our wingèd horse;
This other his helper and friend
Was coming into his force;

He might have won fame in the end,
So sensitive his nature seemed,
So daring and sweet his thought.
This other man I had dreamed
A drunken, vainglorious lout.
He had done most bitter wrong
To some who are near my heart,
Yet I number him in the song;
He, too, has resigned his part
In the casual comedy;
He, too, has been changed in his turn,
Transformed utterly:
A terrible beauty is born.

Hearts with one purpose alone
Through summer and winter seem
Enchanted to a stone
To trouble the living stream.
The horse that comes from the road,
The rider, the birds that range
From cloud to tumbling cloud,
Minute by minute they change;
A shadow of cloud on the stream
Changes minute by minute;
A horse-hoof slides on the brim,
And a horse plashes within it;
The long-legged moor-hens dive,
And hens to moor-cocks call;
Minute by minute they live:
The stone's in the midst of all.

Too long a sacrifice
Can make a stone of the heart.
O when may it suffice?
That in Heaven's part, our part

To murmur name upon name,
As a mother names her child
When sleep at last has come
On limbs that had run wild.
What is it but nightfall?
No, no, not night but death;
Was it needless death after all?
For England may keep faith
For all that is done and said.
We know their dream; enough
To know they dreamed and are dead;
And what if excess of love
Bewildered them till they died?
I write it out in a verse—
MacDonagh and MacBride
And Connolly and Pearse
Now and in time to be,
Wherever green is worn,
Are changed, changed utterly:
A terrible beauty is born.

The 'I' is Yeats himself, for once a poet without a mask. Or is it Yeats wearing his bardic mask? Normally he is far too conscious of our kaleidoscopic rôles as men ('in the course of one revolving moon . . . chymist, fiddler, statesman and buffoon') to use an 'I' which is directly himself. In the Wordsworthian sense, he is the least 'personal' of our poets. But here, he makes a very near approach to the personal—possibly because the theme passionately attracted him, and the bardic rôle was very particularly his own.

'Easter 1916' is about war, but not about the Great War. Yeats was much more interested in the grievances of his fellow Irishmen against England than in the major European conflagration raging at the time. The events described are simple and well known. In the Easter of 1916 a number of men and women died in Dublin, during a famous but premature rising. This poem is Yeats's celebration of them as martyrs to the Irish cause. The poem is not, however, about the justice of their cause, which is played down to a surprising degree—as, indeed, is the very dubious nature of its success. What really interests Yeats about these deaths is the 'terrible beauty' to which they gave birth. The poem is an exploration of the meaning and nature of heroism.

It is a very ambivalent poem as we should expect. The literal meaning is easy enough to grasp, since the whole purpose of the poem is to state it. But there are certain other meanings as well, apparently opposed to the plain literal sense, which one detects in images and symbols, as well as in overtones of a somewhat elusive kind. These secondary 'meanings' are just as fully realised, it is important to notice, as the literal one: to suggest that the poet thinks one thing, but feels another, would be very wide of the mark. In fact, he thinks and feels both. If there *is* a contradiction, it is none of his making. The complexity belongs to life itself, not to his art.

'Easter 1916' is a poem of Yeats's middle period. All the ornateness of his early style has been left behind. At first glance the diction is almost bare, so unobtrusively is every word in its proper place. The words seem indeed to belong together in an indivisible unity, very much like the components of a picture, or of a great building. The poem might almost have been chiselled. In its closing lines Yeats rehearses the names of the dead as a man might carve them, deeply and incisively on stone:

> I write it out in a verse—
> MacDonagh and MacBride
> And Connolly and Pearse
> Now and in time to be . . .

It is as though he is actually gathering these martyrs by his own craftsmanship into 'the artifice of eternity', as he himself asks to be gathered in 'Sailing To Byzantium'. The very austerity of the verse has now become grand and sonorous, to match the full development of its theme.

But the verse is much more flexible than it appears; in the central section of the poem it takes on a remarkably lyrical intensity, to which we must return later. Basically it is a very simple structure, with three stresses in each line. There is a simple but insistent rhyme scheme (a/b/a/b) which supports our sense of the poem as an artifact—something made—rather than as a direct report of experience, even when half-rhymes instead of full rhymes are used. This has much to do with Yeats's approach to war, as a simple comparison with Wilfred Owen shows. In Owen's poems there are assonances and half-rhymes to mirror the waste and incompleteness he records, the pity of war. But in 'Easter 1916' we find full-blooded rhymes, the measured, triumphant progress of the lines—a mirror of glory. It is instructive to scan the lines, and to notice how delicately the metre shifts and moves with the meaning, most of all in the middle section, where the poem's ambivalence is chiefly to be found.

The poem begins descriptively and casually. Yeats has met 'them' as passing acquaintances, and thought next to nothing of it. Dublin is toned down to wintry colouring 'grey/Eighteenth-century houses', and the reference to 'counter or desk' underlines the routine, even dreary nature of the meetings. At this stage he is still the Irish Wit, living in an essentially comic world of passing nods, mocking tales and gibes. He develops his picture of the everyday scene as a 'casual comedy', a world of fools

> Being certain that they and I
> But lived where motley is worn

This is to be contrasted with the heroic world of death and glory, co-existing with the comic world, and waiting to break through —suddenly, totally and irreversibly—as the 'terrible beauty' of the refrain.

This breakthrough is the poem's theme, and it brings Yeats to ground very familiar to him: to the contemplation of a moment *in* time which, by a dramatic and heightened significance, removes itself *out* of time; a moment of choice, or of creation, or of sacrifice when creatures of flesh and blood transcend themselves and their normal lot; when something made or done, some 'awful daring of a moment's surrender', proves more enduring than the creatures who gave it birth.

All of this is foreshadowed in the first appearance of the refrain, after which, however, Yeats returns for a time to his memories. The 'they' of the poem were no saints as the world judges, or as Yeats had reason to judge himself. One was a young man of great promise, one a beautiful woman grown shrewish, one a personal enemy of the poet ('He had done most bitter wrong/To some who are near to my heart'). But good and bad as they may be, in the world of motley, their death removes them all to another dimension. The perspectives of the 'casual comedy' yield to other, and grander perspectives of heroism; all alike are to be numbered in the song.

And so (moving for a moment over the poem's middle section towards its end) the poet celebrates their death, which looms larger and greater than their lives. He does not celebrate, as has already been emphasised, their success in death. Their death did not achieve its aim and might even, Yeats suggests, have been 'needless':

> For England may keep faith
> For all that is done and said. . . .

He celebrates their death as a consummation, an end. It is their willingness to die which has lifted them into the heroic realm, and made them the subject for a song:

> We know their dream; enough
> To know they dreamed and are dead . . .

This, then, is the poem's literal meaning, which so clearly engages the *whole* of the poet's creative energy, his thought and feeling alike. But also, and perhaps necessarily with a theme of this kind, there are other thoughts and feelings awakened by the contemplation of heroic death. There is awareness of waste and decay, of earthly promise sacrificed to one great but frozen moment in time. A memorial may commemorate heroism, but its marble inscription is as cold as the bodies lying beneath. And might it not be better to live, even in our small and motley world, than to lie in grandeur among the dead? Yeats returns many times in his work to this particular point, where his celebration of Art, Intellect, Heroism—the things that are tinged with eternity—is held in tension by an opposing enchantment: of youth, love, transience, 'whatever is begotten, born and dies'. The dilemma is not peculiar to Yeats. Poets always have been, and always will be caught up in the great dialogue between Time and Eternity; in the striving of ecstasy to reach out to permanence, across the gulf inexorably set between them; in the longings of *homo sapiens*, from his agonisingly untenable position between the two, so exactly and memorably described for us by Pope:

> Placed on this Isthmus of a middle state,
> A Being darkly wise, and rudely great:
> With too much knowledge for the Sceptic side,
> With too much weakness for the Stoic's pride,
> He hangs between; in doubt to act, or rest;
> In doubt to deem himself a God, or Beast;
> In doubt his Mind or Body to prefer;
> Born but to die, and reas'ning but to err . . .

Any reader will know the pervasiveness of this theme. A critic, however, will be concerned with the specific occasions when it turns *successfully* into poetry. Most men have experienced at one time or another the great commonplaces of the human predicament; very few have turned such experiences into unique and unforgettable words. It is one such instance we are looking at now. Yeats's refrain is our best clue to the poem's *total* ambivalence, with its fusion of 'terror' and 'beauty' into one new whole. This 'terror' is not simply the terror experienced by the martyrs themselves at their moment of death. It is also, and more importantly, the metaphysical terror with which the rest of us contemplate such a moment, wondering, from inside time and our own mediocrity, was it worth it? Was the exchange of living flesh and blood for this graven glory a fair exchange after all? Our very doubts may be simply cowardice; or they may reach beyond the glory to something too mockingly unanswerable to be borne. The most beautiful moment in the poem comes in its third section, which moves against the literal meaning not in crude statement, but in the delicate suggestiveness of image and symbol. Here, the heroic becomes

> Enchanted to a stone
> To trouble the living stream . . .

and this 'enchantment' links the moment of death with the 'one purpose alone' which led up to it. The whole alchemy, of living men and women transmuted into undying symbols, enters into this image of the stone. But 'stone' is a cold word; and if the stone 'troubles' the living stream, the living stream has warmth and magic of its own. Indeed, the poetry becomes now a celebration of the stream, against which the stone stands out motionless and black, a fitting symbol of the frozen heart. We are caught up in the wonderfully delicate rhythms of life—in the reiterated 'minute by minute', where the movement of horse and cloud and stream link life and transience inextricably together. The movement is too subtle to be pinned down as onomatopoeia, but certainly it enacts its content, offering us the very feel of life.

Here, then, is the world of change and delight; and it is the stone in the centre that strikes chill. The opposition between casual comedy and meaningful heroism is balanced now by this very different opposition, between lilting beauty and the motionless dark:

> Too long a sacrifice
> Can make a stone of the heart . . .

. . . and it is no accident that Yeats sees the singlemindedness of sacrifice leading to death as a 'stone', no less than the death itself. Both are symbolised by the stone, our response to which runs directly counter to the poem as a whole.

The moment you see this, the ambivalence is everywhere apparent. In lines 28-30 it is said of one of the martyrs 'He might have won fame in the end . . .' yet the whole force of the poem appears to be that he *did* win fame in the end. What sort of fame does Yeats hint at here?—some other kind, it seems, than that of life knowing itself sacrificially in one supreme moment of death. And at the end of the poem, the word 'bewildered' is highly significant:

> And what if excess of love
> Bewildered them till they died?

Explicitly, Yeats is saying it doesn't matter: what if they *were* bewildered, he asks? But 'bewildered' and 'died' are strong words, especially with the felt coldness of the stone behind them. Even the image 'To murmur name upon name/As a mother names her child' is not wholly unambiguous. Might the poem be in some sense a lullaby, helping us to forget the dead, even as we honour them?

What one is left feeling is that the poem is a marvellously unified and moving whole. If there *is* a tension of opposites in it, then this is a very faithful reflection of life itself. The poet celebrates heroism finely and memorably, but its enigmas will not be put on one side. And what more can we ask a poet to do? He extends our awareness and sensitivity to life, he makes something new and beautiful for our delight. Ought he to solve the riddles of life as well? There are limits to what we can reasonably expect.

6

BAVARIAN GENTIANS

by D. H. Lawrence

NOT every man has gentians in his house
in Soft September, at slow, Sad Michaelmas.

Bavarian gentians, big and dark, only dark
darkening the day-time torch-like with the smoking blueness
of Pluto's gloom,
ribbed and torch-like, with their blaze of darkness spread blue
down flattening into points, flattened under the sweep of white
day
torch-flower of the blue-smoking darkness, Pluto's dark-blue
daze,
black lamps from the halls of Dio, burning dark blue,
giving off darkness, blue darkness, as Demeter's pale lamps give
off light,
lead me then, lead me the way.

Reach me a gentian, give me a torch
let me guide myself with the blue, forked torch of this flower
down the darker and darker stairs, where blue is darkened on
blueness.
even where Persephone goes, just now, from the frosted September
to the sightless realm where darkness is awake upon the dark
and Persephone herself is but a voice
or a darkness invisible enfolded in the deeper dark

of the arms Plutonic, and pierced with the passion of dense
   gloom,
among the splendour of torches of darkness, shedding darkness
   on the lost bride and her groom.

D. H. Lawrence's verse has aroused much controversy. Some
critics have argued that his loose rhythms, irregular lines and lack
of conventional metrical patterns are really only a kind of dis-
guised prose. In his essay, 'D. H. Lawrence and Expressive Form',
in his book *Language as Gesture* (1954), R. P. Blackmur finds in
Lawrence's verse only 'the ruins of great intentions'. Because
Lawrence thought of his poetry as fragmentary biography, and
relied on the structure of experience itself to provide the structure
of his work, his poems lack any formal principles of organisation.
In Blackmur's view, Lawrence refused to study the craft of the
poet, and as a result his verses, although they include intuitive
flashes of insight, sprawl in confusion across the page. Blackmur's
criticisms have called forth many intelligent replies. Perhaps the
most lucid and sensible account is to be found in Graham
Hough's chapter on Lawrence's poetry in *The Dark Sun* (1956).
Another admirably perceptive defence of Lawrence is V. de
Sola Pinto's article, 'Poet Without a Mask' (*The Critical Quarterly*,
Vol. III, No. 1), though this provoked a vigorous argument with
Henry Gifford, a defender of Blackmur's view.

'Bavarian Gentians' is certainly a great poem. Lawrence's
theories may have led to some bad pieces of writing, but here his
principles of composition are fully justified. His early poems were
modelled on Rossetti, Meredith, Hardy and the Georgians, and
they include diffuse and sentimental passages. About the time of
the Great War, his style changes, and the influences now are
Ezra Pound, the Imagists, Whitman and the Authorised Version
of the Bible. Just as in his novels he developed towards a highly
original type of formal composition, so his poems move towards
the intensely evocative images and rhythms of *Birds, Beasts and*

Flowers (1923) and *Last Poems*, published just after his death. His early novels, for example *Sons and Lovers* (1913), provide superb, full-scale realistic pictures of people and places, in a manner which still in many ways resembles that of Arnold Bennett. In *Women in Love* (1921), he creates a new type of organic form, linking together a series of richly symbolic scenes. In his poetry, he similarly develops a highly personal method of organisation. *Phoenix* (1936) includes a description of the kind of expressive, instantaneous verse he was trying to write. His concern is with 'poetry of that which is at hand: the immediate present. In the immediate present there is no perfection, no consummation, nothing is finished. The strands are all flying, quivering, intermingling into the web, the waters are shaking the moon . . . The living plasm vibrates unspeakably, it inhales the future, it exhales the past. It is the quick of both and yet it is neither.' This description is typically Lawrentian. In his best work he is often striving for expression for difficult, almost mystical, states of mind. He is trying to penetrate beyond normal consciousness to the dark places of the soul. In both fiction and poetry, we often feel a sense of strain, of the style pushing out towards the inexpressible. Orthodox metrical patterns are therefore of no use to him. The organic form of 'Bavarian Gentians', based on repetitions and incantatory rhythms, embodies this 'unspeakable' vibration of the living plasma. The rhetorical phrases without principal verbs, the irregular lines, correspond to this mode of vision. Highly unusual images are repeated in different forms, gradually gaining in evocative power. The emotional surge of the rhythms, close to the prose of the Authorised Version, suggests a religious significance. They are full of sweeping phrases that reflect the soaring of his consciousness into new worlds of experience. Of his rhythms, he wrote: 'I think I read my poetry more by length than by stress—as a matter of movements in space than footsteps hitting the earth . . . I think more of a bird with broad wings flying and lapsing through the air more than anything, when I think of metre . . . It all depends on the pause, the natural pause, the natural lingering of the voice according to the feeling.' He constantly revised his verses in order to achieve the rhythmic effects he wanted. Far from writing turgid, uninspired free verse, he developed a new kind of poetic expression, recreating the richness and resonance of the Authorised Version of the Song of Songs, or the Psalms.

Graham Hough points out how difficult it is to analyse this unique verse of Lawrence: 'When poetry succeeds formally its quality can be fully exposed by formal criticism; all has been manifested in form. When poetry partly fails from a formal point of view, yet something impressive remains, formal criticism can never be enough.' In discussing Lawrence's poetry, we are thrown back on biographical details, and on an attempt to re-express the poem in words of our own. 'Bavarian Gentians' was written when Lawrence was in the South of France just before he died. Its mood is that of his great poem 'The Ship of Death', and his last story, *The Man Who Died*. In these works, Lawrence is very conscious of his own approaching death. The line 'in Soft September, at slow, Sad Michaelmas' beautifully expresses his resignation, his melancholy acceptance of the passing away of all living things. In 'Bavarian Gentians', he is not concerned, as in earlier poems, to give the reader an immediate apprehension of the life of the flowers, but uses them as a symbol of ultimate mysteries. He interprets the Greek myth of Pluto and Persephone in his own way, using images of gentians and the underworld to express personal attitudes towards death. He feels no anguish at the loss of life. Like Persephone, he will be embraced by death as by a lover. The poem is a supreme expression of Lawrence's mystical conception of sex. The gods in whom he believed are part of the natural processes of life. In death he will be united with them, and he talks of this with controlled sensuousness. This apprehension of death, calm, courageous and almost joyful, is beyond rational analysis. The poem creates its own mixture of sensuous and mystical apprehension, and the analytical critic, even more than usual, must recognise his inadequacy.

The images of darkness, repeated in the form of an incantation, make death appear frightening. We too must one day follow the path 'down the darker and darker stairs'. But this darkness is not seen as complete negation. The 'blue-smoking' gentians symbolise a power of life which will exist even in death. Guided by their beauty, Lawrence will walk with confidence into the underworld. But the darkness is too much 'the sightless realm', an area of 'gloom', for this to be a completely joyful poem. Conflicting emotions struggle for expression. Death is both negation and fulfilment. There is a sadness, a feeling of inevitable movement towards the land of cold shades, where live 'the lost bride and her groom'; and yet there is also exaltation, as if Lawrence is participating in some initiation rite. 'The Ship of Death' expresses the same paradox. In the opening lines, death is oblivion, and this word is repeated with great emphasis:

> Now it is autumn and the falling fruit
> and the long journey towards oblivion.

But towards the end of the poem dawn comes again, and 'the body, like a worn sea-shell emerges strange and lovely'. So in 'Bavarian Gentians' we remember that each Spring Persephone returns to the world of light and colour.

The imagery of 'Bavarian Gentians' creates this double effect throughout the poem. Phrases such as 'blaze of darkness', 'black lamps' and 'darkness is awake upon the dark' create a sense of living darkness, a mysterious, passionate life more vital than anything in this daylight world. The various images of light, the 'blaze', 'torch' and 'lamp' heighten the sense of darkness by contrast. We feel the darkness envelop us like a flood of seawater at night, yet in the deeper dark await the arms Plutonic, promising some ultimate kind of fulfilment.

'Lead me then, lead me the way', asks Lawrence. As in all his art, life is a search for completeness. Now he enters Pluto's 'dark-blue daze'. This image, recalling 'blaze' in a previous line, suggests wonder and amazement. He is journeying into 'blue darkness', and this symbolises the paradox of the poem. Throughout his life Lawrence sought for rebirth, for heroic fulfilment in this world, but he could not conquer pain and evil. There are growing signs of despair in his later work, and often he seems to be moving towards a rejection of this world and all its compromises. Sex becomes involved in religious mysticism, as in *The Man Who Died*, or part of an Arcadian idyll, as in *Lady Chatterley's Lover*. He becomes less and less concerned with the realities of the flesh as an end in themselves. So in 'Bavarian Gentians', the symbols embody his final apprehensions of life and death, his longing for rebirth and his fear of oblivion. He goes into death like Persephone to Pluto, august, god-like, embraced by a darkness beyond comprehension.

7

MARINA *by T. S. Eliot*

Quis hic locus, quae
regio, quae mundi plaga?

WHAT seas what shores what grey rocks and what islands
What water lapping the bow
And scent of pine and the woodthrush singing through the fog
What images return
O my daughter.

Those who sharpen the tooth of the dog, meaning
Death
Those who glitter with the glory of the hummingbird, meaning
Death
Those who sit in the stye of contentment, meaning
Death
Those who suffer the ecstasy of the animals, meaning
Death

Are become unsubstantial, reduced by a wind,
A breath of pine, and the woodsong fog
By this grace dissolved in place

What is this face, less clear and clearer
The pulse in the arm, less strong and stronger—
Given or lent? more distant than stars and nearer than the eye

Whispers and small laughter between leaves and hurrying feet
Under sleep, where all the waters meet.

Bowsprit cracked with ice and paint cracked with heat.
I made this, I have forgotten
And remember.
The rigging weak and the canvas rotten
Between one June and another September.
Made this unknowing, half conscious, unknown, my own.
The garboard strake leaks, the seams need caulking.
This form, this face, this life
Living to live in a world of time beyond me; let me
Resign my life for this life, my speech for that unspoken,
The awakened, lips parted, the hope, the new ships.

What seas what shores what granite islands towards my timbers
And woodthrush calling through the fog
My daughter.

In an address given at Edinburgh University in 1937, Eliot
said that 'the finest of all "recognition scenes" is Act V. i. of that
very great play, *Pericles*. It is a perfect example of the "ultra-
dramatic", a dramatic action of beings who are more than
human. . . . It is the speech of creatures who are more than
human, or rather, seen in a light more than that of day.' In
Shakespeare's play, Pericles had believed his daughter, Marina,
was dead, and only at the end is she restored to him. He is overcome with amazement, feeling that his discovery of the lost
child must be an hallucination, 'the rarest dream that e'er dull
sleep did mock sad fools withal.' Eliot's poem is about his own
search for religious experience, and about a moment of discovery,
when the lost innocence seems to be found again. The story of
Pericles and Marina is used as a means of describing Eliot's own
experience of illumination. But the poem's epigraph indicates
that this is no poem of simple faith. The words 'Quis hic locus,
quae regio, quae mundi plaga?' are spoken by Hercules in
Seneca's play, *Hercules Furens*. Hercules has slaughtered his own

73

children in a fit of madness, and, now returning to sanity, is questioning where he is and what he has done. Eliot's poem is full of questions, for he is uncertain whether his moment of illumination is a real contact with the living God or an illusion of the senses. Can he regain the lost innocence, represented by Marina, or has this been killed by himself long ago?

The greatness of Eliot's religious poetry derives from its scrupulously honest depiction of his own states of mind, its precise analysis of his indecisive religious apprehensions. In 'Tintern Abbey', Wordsworth describes his response to Nature:

> And I have felt
> A presence that disturbs me with the joy
> Of elevated thoughts; a sense sublime
> Of something far more deeply interfused
> Whose dwelling is the light of setting suns,
> And the round ocean and the living air,
> And the blue sky, and in the mind of man:

The word 'something' describes most precisely his sense that some meaning exists in the beauty of Nature, even though he cannot define this more exactly. He can only be true to his own experience. Eliot is similarly completely honest in recording his own uncertainties. His religious poetry can be appreciated by both believers and non-believers because his apprehensions are so beautifully and subtly observed. This is seen in 'Marina', and of course, in *Four Quartets*.

In the first six lines, Pericles is recalling his journey. It is as if he were in a boat in a fog, so close to an island that he can smell the pine and hear the woodthrush singing. This is a beautiful image for Eliot's own religious awareness. Normal day-to-day apprehension is like a fog, but occasionally we feel that just beyond our sense there is land, a different order of reality. Intimations of immortality, the scent of pine and a woodthrush singing, make this island seem of breathtaking loveliness; yet there is also fear, for we may be wrecked upon the grey rocks. The divine lies behind a fog, and we can never achieve certain knowledge; yet we all know moments of time when we feel that, if only we could grasp it, something of great beauty and significance lies just outside the perimeter of human consciousness. This knowledge brings fear, for the new order of reality may upset all our old presuppositions.

The lack of grammar in these lines makes them appear part of a dream-like reflection. Is Pericles awake or asleep? The cadences move slowly, with lyrical grace, as if Pericles is savouring all the delight of his discovery. In Eliot's poetry, such sequences of images linked together without the relationships imposed by ordinary syntax, provide a uniquely original form of poetry. His conception of the image, discussed in our introduction, determines the construction of the poem. Understanding of these images grows as we read more of Eliot's verse, particularly the other Ariel poems, *Ash Wednesday* and *Four Quartets*.

The purpose of the images in 'Marina' is not to analyse religious experience into a series of logical or dogmatic statements, but to reflect a state of mind. In his essays and poems, Eliot asserts that knowledge exists only in the individual consciousness, and that to formulate logical sequences of words in syntactical forms is to move one step away from reality: 'Language in a healthy state presents the object, is so close to the object, that the two are identified.' If this is so, then language must move through time in the same manner as the living mind. Eliot repeatedly talks about the way we are born and die in each moment. The person who read the first sentence of this description of 'Marina' a few seconds ago is dead, an unchangeable part of history. This sense of constant movement in the individual consciousness is described by the Unidentified Guest in *The Cocktail Party*:

Ah, but we die to each other daily.
What we know of other people
Is only our memory of the moments
During which we knew them. And they have changed
          since then.
To pretend that they and we are the same
Is a useful and convenient social convention
Which must sometimes be broken. We must also
          remember
That at every meeting we are meeting a stranger.
          (Act I, sc. iii)

In his religious poetry, particularly *Four Quartets*, Eliot looks for connections between past, present and future, for a still point in the centre of the wheel of time; but he does not find this through a rational series of arguments, in the manner of a philosopher or theologian. Instead of syntactical arrangements of ideas, his poetry offers interrelated images, interrelated themes, out of which the assertions of *Little Gidding* can be made. In 'Marina', he is trying to create a series of images that mime Pericles's state of mind, and thereby reflect his own experience of illumination. But Eliot thinks that this 'miming' cannot be achieved in a dramatic action, with a beginning, middle and end, with subjects governing verbs, all arranged in a grammatical order. Unsure of the exact relationships between the parts of his experience, he can reflect only the shifting emotions and ideas that pass through his mind. The philosophical attitudes behind these ideas are explained in detail in Helen Gardner's *The Art of T. S. Eliot* and Hugh Kenner's *The Invisible Poet*. Eliot seeks for new forms which can adequately reflect the individual consciousness, and, in his religious poetry, he tries to discover pattern in the movements of the mind.

After the first five lines, recalling the journey, Pericles describes the effects of the illumination brought to him by Marina.

The 'death-in-life' world of *The Waste Land* becomes unsubstantial. Pericles lists all the forms of evil that now are without substance. Those who sharpen the tooth of the dog are the warmongers, those who glitter with the glory of the hummingbird are the vain and the proud, those who sit in the stye of contentment are the self-deceived, with no sense of sin, those who suffer the ecstasy of the animals are the lustful. The chant-like arrangement of the words emphasises that all these activities are forms of death. The wind from the island, wafting pine-scent, the woodsong drifting out in the fog, reveal to Pericles a vision of divine beauty that reduces ordinary human sins to their true proportions. The word 'grace' hints at a possible Christian interpretation. The Grace of God comes to Pericles, not as an abstract concept, but dissolved in a particular place, known here through the discovery of his child. So all believers receive Grace not as an idea, but through some person or event at some particular place. But all these images are elusive, full of hints and indecisions, and no precise interpretation is possible. There is no full stop after 'place' because the experience is continuing, and may not be defined clearly. It cannot be expressed in the order of a sentence. So the next three lines are full of questions. Pericles is losing himself in his dream, almost turning the real Marina into a figment of his imagination. He is overwhelmed by the vision of innocence revealed in Marina. As he swoons, the physical face becomes less clear, but the symbolic face, the spiritual illumination, becomes clearer. Although his own physical body is fainting, overcome by amazement, his spiritual health is stronger. And where does this experience come from? Has someone—God, perhaps—given it to him? Or lent it so that later it must be returned in some form? The conclusion of these three lines marvellously represents the ambiguities of religious experience, the sense that God is both more distant than stars and yet, at other times, within our very minds. Once more these lines do not end with a full stop, for nothing is concluded here.

The next two lines:

Whispers and small laughter between leaves and hurrying feet
Under sleep, where all the waters meet.

repeat an image of childhood innocence which Eliot uses in his
short lyric, 'New Hampshire', and, much more subtly, in *Four
Quartets*. The narrator apprehends innocence like a man sitting
in an orchard, hearing the whispers and laughter of children
behind the trees. Like the image of the island in the fog, the
whispers suggest that religious experience is always beyond
grasp, heard, half-heard, between two waves of the sea. 'Under
sleep' reminds us of the dreamlike quality of the experience.
Here our individual rivers join the ocean, and the journey of life
is ended. But this line is particularly elusive. All sorts of memories
crowd in. Perhaps the waters meet in the ocean of God, the sea
of eternity. And yet other possibilities cannot be ignored. We
remember psychological interpretations of the oceanic impulse,
the desire to renounce individuality and return to the womb.
These words reflect a state of mind, and offer no interpretation.

After these ambiguous lines, Pericles recalls the hardships of his
journey, the ice and the heat. The words look forward to ideas
examined again in *Four Quartets*. The search for innocence is
something he has 'made' by his journeys. But the effort, even
perhaps the discovery itself, is for a few moments only, and when
it is finished, the journey must begin again: 'Old men ought to
be explorers'. What he has discovered, once the experience is
over, he can never be certain about. Between September and
June may be a nine-month period before a real birth, but the
arrangement of the words is deliberately obscure. Yet the poem,
with its many lines of beauty and wonder, is not without
assertions. The unknown must remain beyond complete apprehension, a reality of which we are half-conscious; yet there
are moments when Pericles makes this new world his own. And
this line is concluded by a full stop.

The boat, the physical body, has its weaknesses; but Pericles, in words which still have their hesitations, moves at the end towards hope. He wants to resign his life for the vision. He asserts that this is no dream, but an awakening, a rebirth. The end of this section suggests that he will have to journey again in 'the new ships', but these words move towards a climax followed again by a full stop. He accepts the moment of illumination as real. So in the last three lines he knows that Marina, the divine, lost innocence of the Garden of Eden, is waiting behind the fog. Phrases from the beginning of the poem are repeated, but now the woodthrush calls 'My daughter'.

8

THE LANDSCAPE
NEAR AN AERODROME

by Stephen Spender

MORE beautiful and soft than any moth
With burring furred antennae feeling its huge path
Through dusk, the air liner with shut-off engines
Glides over suburbs and the sleeves set trailing tall
To point the wind. Gently, broadly, she falls,
Scarcely disturbing charted currents of air.

Lulled by descent, the travellers across sea
And across feminine land indulging its easy limbs
In miles of softness, now let their eyes trained by watching
Penetrate through dusk the outskirts of this town
Here where industry shows a fraying edge.
Here they may see what is being done.

Beyond the winking masthead light
And the landing ground, they observe the outposts
Of work: chimneys like lank black fingers
Or figures, frightening and mad: and squat buildings
With their strange air behind trees, like women's faces
Shattered by grief. Here where few houses
Moan with faint light behind their blinds,
They remark the unhomely sense of complaint, like a dog
Shut out, and shivering at the foreign moon.

In the last sweep of love, they pass over fields
Behind the aerodrome, where boys play all day
Hacking dead grass: whose cries, like wild birds,
Settle upon the nearest roofs
But soon are hid under the loud city.

Then, as they land, they hear the tolling bell
Reaching across the landscape of hysteria,
To where, louder than all those batteries
And charcoaled towers against that dying sky,
Religion stands, the Church blocking the sun.

Together with W. H. Auden, C. Day Lewis and Louis MacNeice, Spender was one of the 'New Country' group, whose verse was published in *New Signatures*, 1932 and *New Country*, 1933. These poets believed that they should be involved in contemporary life, and actively engaged in politics. In 'The Funeral', Spender exults in the approaching triumph of Communism:

They speak of the World State
With its towns like brain centres and its pulsing arteries.

He tries to believe in the future, delighting in man's success in conquering Nature. He wrote with enthusiasm of electric pylons, or of an express train at night:

. . . like a comet through flames she moves entranced
Wrapt in her music no bird song, no, nor bough
Breaking with honey buds, shall ever equal.

Such deliberate use of imagery taken from machinery, together with optimistic Communism, brought him notoriety in the 1930's; but he was straining against his own true instincts. He was never a true Marxist, but a romantic liberal, longing for a new age of heroism. What he saw around him in the world of the 1930's made him increasingly melancholy and pessimistic. His optimistic passages sound contrived, and his best poems express sad compassion for those who must live surrounded by the ugliness of the modern town.

'The Landscape Near An Aerodrome' expresses very poignantly this conflict of attitudes. The poem puts before us two very different pictures. The aeroplane, beautiful and free as it floats gently towards the town, is contrasted with the chimneys and factories, the landscape of hysteria. An aeroplane is a symbol of man's conquest of the air, and the advance of science; it recalls those pre-1914 humanist dreams of writers such as H. G. Wells, who thought men were about to create better and better worlds. For Spender, it is still an object of beauty, free of the bonds that hold men down to the earth. But the first line compares the aeroplane to a moth, and immediately the freedom of the aeroplane appears flimsy, something easily broken. As the plane descends, it is as if it is being drawn down into the nightmare landscape, and, like the cries of the boys, will soon be hidden by the city. The picture of the aeroplane is most beautifully developed. The slow movement of the verse—'gently, broadly, she falls'—mimes the quiet descent of the plane. There is something almost unreal about this huge air-liner, scarcely disturbing the air as it floats downwards, and the travellers themselves are nearly lulled to sleep by its motion. The whole picture is of a fragile beauty, almost dream-like, being drawn to the town, just as Spender's own optimism was brought into contact with the social realities of his times. The plane has travelled across 'feminine land indulging its easy limbs, In miles of softness'. It is easy to indulge in dreams of progress, but they are perhaps an escape from the masculine world of action. The travellers peer down at the suburbs, for here 'they may see what is being done.'

Spender's conflict between faith in progress and romantic nostalgia is paralleled by contrasting uses of imagery. Influenced by Donne, he tries to be exact and precise, and to use startling comparisons, but instinctively he prefers the evocative imagery of Shelley. The third section of the poem tries to give a realistic picture of an industrialised landscape, but this turns into a strange nightmare. The construction of the sentences indicates that the travellers are supposed to be unbiassed observers, with a clinical detachment. We are told that 'they observe', 'they remark', as if they are taking notes. But the images themselves are highly evocative, almost like a description from a Gothic melodrama. The chimneys are like lank, black fingers, as if some giant were buried here. The description of 'figures frightening and mad' does not have much to do with chimneys, but suggests some kind of hysterical dance. This is followed by a most ambiguous image, which must arouse different associations in each reader. Presumably the trees stand before the squat buildings as heavy lines of grief cover an old woman's face; but, as we read this poem, we do not work out the comparison exactly, but respond to its emotional effects. 'Squat buildings' with their 'strange' air behind trees suggest mystery, and perhaps even a certain beauty. The comparison with the woman is too far-fetched to add to this picture of the buildings; instead we are likely to visualise large, grief-stricken faces of women peering through dark trees, as in some surrealist painting. In the final lines of this section, two ideas are again violently and not very precisely yoked together. It is difficult to see why faint light behind blinds should bring to mind the complaining of a dog. To many people the lights of a city at dusk suggest warmth, comfort and home.

This whole section depicts with considerable emotional force Spender's own despair; but it would be more successful if the images of grief were not so arbitrarily linked with the buildings. Instead of a realistic picture of a squalid landscape, this is the nightmare of a romantic, reacting violently from the ugliness of life. For the rest of the poem, sadness predominates. A highly evocative image gives us a last glimpse of the aeroplane, sweeping down as if in love with the earth, and passing over the boys, whose natural joy is part of the aeroplane's free world. But the boys hack dead grass in suburbia, and their freedom will soon be ended. As the plane lands, the travellers hear the church bells. For Spender, these are symbols of repression, of outworn creeds which prevent people from living full and beautiful lives. The poem ends with the church towers blocking out the sunlight from this stricken town.

This is a good poem, but not so great as some of the others printed in this book. The images of the town are too hysterical, and the rhythms do not have that distinctive, personal quality that one always finds in Eliot or Yeats. The lines have various numbers of syllables, but there are usually the regular number of five stresses. Spender adapts this form of free verse to his own requirements. Additional stressed syllables are included in the second and fourth line to indicate the slow, floating movement of the aeroplane; and in the last line 'Church' and 'block' are heavily stressed together, to mime the burden of religion on the people. The stresses create two tones of voice to suit the world of the aeroplane and the town. A tone of sadness alternates with an almost melodramatic energy. Spender feels horror at the black, deadened lives of the townspeople; his response is a nostalgic longing for a dreamlike freedom, for the natural life of childhood, the boys shouting together 'like wild birds'.

9

SNOW *by Louis MacNeice*

THE room was suddenly rich and the great bay-window was
Spawning snow and pink roses against it
Soundlessly collateral and incompatible:
World is suddener than we fancy it.

World is crazier and more of it than we think,
Incorrigibly plural. I peel and portion
A tangerine and spit the pips and feel
The drunkenness of things being various.

And the fire flames with a bubbling sound for world
Is more spiteful and gay than one supposes—
On the tongue on the eyes on the ears in the palms of one's
    hands—
There is more than glass between the snow and the huge roses.

'The room was suddenly rich' . . . The 'suddenly' captures that
sense of unheralded insight, a sharp tang of delight, which makes
a moment permanently memorable. We have all had such
moments, many of them reaching back to childhood. They
remain in the mind like portraits in a long, dark gallery, waiting
for the chance smell, or word, or sound which will light them
again. They come back to us with nostalgia and poignancy;
often with the suggestion of some close approach to greater
realities, a 'near annunciation', to borrow Day Lewis's phrase.
The world is irradiated with an unfamiliar brilliance. Memory,
of course, alters as it recalls, but when such moments happen,

and afterwards when they come back to us, they are marked by their peculiar intensity, of a sharply sensuous kind.

Such moments have their diversity, their own classic problems of interpretation. A 'Proustian moment' we say—and the psychological ramifications, steeped in nostalgia, are very likely what we have in mind. Or we may call them 'spots of time', recalling Wordsworth's numinous insights, the 'rememberable things' upon which his poetic and religious hopes came increasingly to depend. T. S. Eliot's *Four Quartets* is a modern *locus classicus* among poems where numinous moments have supreme and haunting importance. So, in their diverse and perhaps smaller ways are at least two of the other poems in this present collection—Dylan Thomas's 'Fern Hill' and C. Day Lewis's 'O Dreams, O Destinations'.

The distinguishing characteristic of these moments is that they are not caused by anything; they are not moments when the facts of (say) love, or death, are powerfully brought home to us in our own experience. On the contrary, they overtake us suddenly and inexplicably, as in 'Snow'. There is no rational explanation of them. They haunt us with significances beyond anything we feel could be rationally explained, whether we also think of them as 'mystical' or not.

How does MacNeice treat such a moment in 'Snow'? Certainly not mystically, though the sense of *mystery* is not lacking. It is almost like a conjuring trick: the poet waves his wand, and hey presto!—the whole room lights up, like a Christmas tree seen by a child. But the magic and the gaiety are real enough: the trick is one of life's tricks, not the poet's: there is no disappointing legerdemain going on behind the scenes. What we are conscious of is the immediacy of the illumination. It is not mediated to us second-hand, whether through memory, or reflection, or theory, or some need it is co-opted to fulfil. There is no nostalgia surrounding it; it just happens, with a sensuous shock we are made to feel to the full.

MacNeice is not alone among the poets of the Thirties in his sensitivity to heightened moments. They were all very youthful poets ('poets exploding like bombs', says Auden in 'Spain'); their intense vitality was threatened, and therefore intensified, by the political menace in the air. At any second the magic might work backwards, the charm dissolve in illusion, the light fade as suddenly as it appeared. One remembers another of Louis MacNeice's poems, where life and gaiety are switched off even as we look:

> The sunlight on the garden
> Hardens and grows cold,
> We cannot cage the minute
> Within its nets of gold . . .

But there is no menace in 'Snow', and fittingly, for its magic is of an especially Christmas-like kind. Nor is the moment laden with any obviously intrusive symbolism. Clearly we are in the presence of a real experience, of something which happened to the poet in one place and at one time; the roses are roses, and the snow is snow. Inevitably, there *are* symbolic overtones as well. The theme makes it necessary that there should be. Whenever we catch apparent opposites co-existing with one another, in defiance of all the rules for them we should like to make, symbolic overtones are bound to be heard. But these overtones are not what the poem is about, and indeed if they were, there would be little of real interest to hold us enthralled. The scene is best visualised on its own terms before any kind of symbolism is allowed to appear. The snow is on the outside of the 'great bay window', spattering it; the great bowl of roses is inside, standing in front of the window on a table or pedestal of some kind. The tangerines are in a fruit bowl, and the fire has been very recently mended with logs. The snow and the roses appear to belong at opposite poles to each other (winter and summer, white and red) but they are brought into conjunction as a matter of fact: 'Soundlessly collateral and incompatible'.

Two sharply different worlds are juxtaposed, and no answer is given to suggest why they are. Indeed, there is not even a question, though one feels the excitement of the event. In a sense, there may seem little to explain. Surely half the houses in the country could show the same Christmas décor, flowers and snow separated by a thinly invisible sheet of glass? But this is not what the poet feels as he looks at them. 'There is more than glass between the snow and the huge roses': there is the mysteriousness of the things themselves, usually overlooked in the dullness of familiar vision; there is the mysteriousness of their co-existence, not only through the glass, but in the universe; in the fantastic diversity and economy of creation itself.

What the poem really offers is a release of possibilities, a lifting of our minds and spirits out of the normal rut. Familiar things become exciting again, familiar conjunctions become as strange and inexplicable as they really are. For a moment we look up from our cramped and pigeon-holed universe, catching a glimpse of the almost forgotten vistas outside:

> World is crazier and more of it than we think,
> Incorrigibly plural.

Yet it is still an impish, a social world that we see, a crazy world, more than a little mad. The imagery is lively and festive, drawn from natural fecundity ('Spawning', 'bubbling') and human conviviality ('drunkenness', 'gay'). It is imagery with hints of danger in it as well: fecundity and drunkenness can get out of hand, gaiety cannot always be trusted behind your back. The 'spiteful and gay' suggests a gossipy liveliness, a Walpolian or Shavian universe, where everything is sparkling and barbed.

Louis MacNeice delights in this sparkle—a cosmic blarney almost, stretching all of our senses at once. There is pleasure for the sight, in visual clarity; for the taste and touch ('I peel and portion A tangerine and spit the pips'); for the hearing ('a bubbling sound'). These pleasures echo in the poem's brisk onomatopoeia, and are caught up in its penultimate line:

> On the tongue on the eyes on the ears in the palms of one's hands . . .

The real purpose of the poem is in fact evocative. Louis MacNeice is not recording excitement, he is communicating it; the words he uses are part of the excitement; we are caught up in it ourselves. The captured moment exists not for anything it points towards, but for what it actually is. 'Suddener', 'crazier', 'more of it', 'incorrigibly plural', 'rich'. It is like a stage set as the curtain rises, before the players have had time to appear. It is like the sudden exhilarations of a child, transcending any cause or effect one can clearly discern.

The poem's impishness is neither religious nor social; it is personal, an overflowing of vitality in response to the vitality of creation itself. The vision of the snow and the huge roses is indeed a revelation, but a revelation of what we can feel. We are offered a liberating vision of the intensity and diversity of things; of the real possibility of joy.

10

SPAIN 1937 *by W. H. Auden*

YESTERDAY all the past. The language of size
Spreading to China along the trade-routes; the diffusion
        Of the counting-frame and the cromlech;
Yesterday the shadow-reckoning in the sunny climates.

Yesterday the assessment of insurance by cards,
The divination of water; yesterday the invention
        Of cart-wheels and clocks, the taming of
Horses; yesterday the bustling world of navigators.

Yesterday the abolition of fairies and giants;
The fortress like a motionless eagle eyeing the valley,
        The chapel built in the forest;
Yesterday the carving of angels and of frightening gargoyles.

The trial of heretics among the columns of stone;
Yesterday the theological feuds in the taverns
        And the miraculous cure at the fountain;
Yesterday the Sabbath of Witches. But to-day the struggle.

Yesterday the installation of dynamos and turbines;
The construction of railways in the colonial desert;
        Yesterday the classic lecture
On the origin of Mankind. But to-day the struggle.

Yesterday the belief in the absolute value of Greek;
The fall of the curtain upon the death of a hero;
        Yesterday the prayer to the sunset,
And the adoration of madmen. But to-day the struggle.

As the poet whispers, startled among the pines
Or, where the loose waterfall sings, compact, or upright
    On the crag by the leaning tower:
'O my vision. O send me the luck of the sailor.'

And the investigator peers through his instruments
At the inhuman provinces, the virile bacillus
    Or enormous Jupiter finished:
'But the lives of my friends. I inquire, I inquire.'

And the poor in their fireless lodgings dropping the sheets
Of the evening paper: 'Our day is our loss. O show us
    History the operator, the
Organizer, Time the refreshing river.'

And the nations combine each cry, invoking the life
That shapes the individual belly and orders
    The private nocturnal terror:
'Did you not found once the city state of the sponge,

'Raise the vast military empires of the shark
And the tiger, establish the robin's plucky canton?
    Intervene, O descend as a dove or
A furious papa or a mild engineer: but descend.'

And the life, if it answers at all, replies from the heart
And the eyes and the lungs, from the shops and squares of the city:
    'O no, I am not the Mover,
Not to-day, not to you. To you I'm the

'Yes-man, the bar-companion, the easily-duped:
I am whatever you do; I am your vow to be
    Good, your humorous story;
I am your business voice; I am your marriage.

'What's your proposal? To build the Just City? I will.
I agree. Or is it the suicide pact, the romantic
    Death? Very well, I accept, for
I am your choice, your decision: yes, I am Spain.'

Many have heard it on remote peninsulas,
On sleepy plains, in the aberrant fishermen's islands,
  In the corrupt heart of the city;
Have heard and migrated like gulls or the seeds of a flower.

They clung like burrs to the long expresses that lurch
Through the unjust lands, through the night, through the alpine
 tunnel;
  They floated over the oceans;
They walked the passes: they came to present their lives.

On that arid square, that fragment nipped off from hot
Africa, soldered so crudely to inventive Europe,
  On that tableland scored by rivers,
Our fever's menacing shapes are precise and alive.

To-morrow, perhaps, the future: the research on fatigue
And the movements of packers; the gradual exploring of all the
  Octaves of radiation;
To-morrow the enlarging of consciousness by diet and breathing.

To-morrow the rediscovery of romantic love;
The photographing of ravens; all the fun under
  Liberty's masterful shadow;
To-morrow the hour of the pageant-master and the musician.

To-morrow, for the young, the poets exploding like bombs,
The walks by the lake, the winter of perfect communion;
  To-morrow the bicycle races
Through the suburbs on summer evenings: but to-day the
 struggle.

To-day the inevitable increase in the chances of death,
The conscious acceptance of guilt in the fact of murder;
  To-day the expending of powers
On the flat ephemeral pamphlet and the boring meeting.

To-day the makeshift consolations; the shared cigarette;
The cards in the candle-lit barn and the scraping concert,
      The masculine jokes; to-day the
Fumbled and unsatisfactory embrace before hurting.

The stars are dead; the animals will not look:
We are left alone with our day, and the time is short and
      History to the defeated
May say Alas but cannot help or pardon.

This is perhaps the most celebrated of all the poems of the
1930's, for it gave striking artistic form to the instinctive apprehensions of a whole generation of young men and women. It is
difficult for those born since the Thirties to imagine the importance of the Spanish Civil War to the minds of the intellectuals
of the time. Its effect was comparable to that of the French
Revolution on young writers such as Wordsworth and Coleridge. The poem originally sold as a pamphlet at a shilling, the
author's royalties being given to 'Medical Aid for Spain'. It was
one of those rare occasions in the twentieth century when an
important poet found popular expression for the public feelings
of his age.

As a poet, Auden has always been very conscious of both
economic conflicts in England, and wider international affairs.
Inspired by a powerful sense of social commitment, he was
convinced that the artist must play his part in politics: 'we are
the conscripts of our age'. He did not wish to be only a personal
voice, speaking to a small élite, but wanted to have a positive
effect on the great conflicts of the pre-1939 world. For him, 'no
policy of isolation is possible'. He sought for some kind of
positive action to resolve 'our fever's menacing shapes', and the
Spanish Civil War at last seemed to provide him with his
opportunity.

Auden's attitude to Spain is by no means as naïve as the

theatrical refrains of the poem might suggest. For Auden, Spain was a symbol of the political, cultural and imaginative conflicts of his age. Like all politically-conscious men of his generation, he felt a sense of approaching disaster, as Mussolini and Hitler spread their power across Europe. But Auden was aware of deeper implications to the struggle. Since the 1914-18 war, Western civilisation had moved from one crisis to the next. The left-wing dreams of a utopian future were confronted by a nightmare vision of evil. Were the ideals of any of the reformers, whether Socialists, Fabians or Marxists, capable of realisation? In the Thirties, intellectuals could still believe in the future, and hope that through political action their causes would be successful. But Auden, supremely sensitive to the temper of the age, was not blind to the naïvety of such idealists. There was in him a strong vein of scepticism that undermined his self-confidence. The conflict between Fascism and Marxism, between optimism and pessimism, was linked to his preoccupations as an artist. In the preceding decades, poets had become increasingly isolated, often viewing with despair, as Eliot did, the contemporary wasteland. Auden felt he must resist the forces driving him into a similar position. He must prevent society from turning the artist into the exception, a voice crying in the wilderness. Before 1937 he tried various experiments in verse to deal with these problems. For him, the Spanish Civil War made both his own and international conflicts 'precise and alive'. Now was the time to act if Western civilisation was to be preserved from final decay. Now was the time to act if art was to be saved from an effete scepticism. Spain was the last chance to redeem the optimistic social reformers' faith in the future. If they should fail, 'History to the defeated May say Alas but cannot help or pardon.'

Auden's attempts to write a public type of verse were fraught with technical difficulties. In contrast to Kipling or Chesterton, he could not feel any sense of community with the majority of the reading public. Born into a middle-class home, trained at

Oxford, he had not the kind of imagination needed to understand the consciousness of the workers whose cause he championed. In his search for a style, he moved rapidly from one type of verse to the next, now preaching dogmatically with naïve fervour, now composing exquisite lyrics to mirror his own uncertainties. 'Spain 1937' does not completely solve these problems. The refrain 'but to-day the struggle' is a little too melodramatic, and the images are unequal in their effects. Some are very successful. The lines:

> On that arid square, that fragment nipped off from hot
> Africa, soldered so crudely to inventive Europe,
>> On that tableland scored by rivers,
> Our fever's menacing shapes are precise and alive

are generally reckoned to be among the best that Auden has written. Instead of treating Nature in a romantic, Wordsworthian manner, he perceives the importance of geographical patterns, and how these are relevant to economic, political or social problems. Spain, 'that arid square', is African in temperament and climate, yet here must be fought out the conflicts of the West. But after this stanza there are many unsatisfactory images. 'The shared cigarette', 'the masculine joke', and 'the Fumbled and unsatisfactory embrace before hurting' are all banal. We feel that Auden is trying to share the temperament of the ordinary soldier, but that his mind cannot escape from clichés. The whole poem is written in different tones of voice. Some parts, particularly the central section, are quite difficult to understand, and could never have a wide appeal. At other times the rhetoric is strained, and we do not feel this voice speaks confidently for a large community.

Yet the poem is full of vitality and energy. The first six stanzas create a vivid sense of the abundance of human activities in the past. We feel the power of the human race, the force and intelligence that makes civilisation, spreading out along the trade-routes, extending its control of environment through the advances of science. But the images are not all taken from the bustling world of commerce and exploration. We are reminded in a most striking image of warfare—'The fortress like a motionless eagle eyeing the valley'—and of superstition. In the opening stanza, 'the counting-frame and the cromlech' symbolise the conflict that the Spanish Civil War may resolve. Science and superstition have developed together. Will the Civil War signalise the final triumph of progress or of the forces of evil? Today the question may seem ironic. But in the Thirties world government and eternal peace still seemed an immanent possibility. All these illustrations are intended to provide objective pictures of the past, and so they offer little in themselves to practical analysis; but as a whole they sum up Auden's view of the significant conflicts of his time. It is perhaps a sign of his insight that he ends this section pessimistically with 'the prayer to the sunset, And the adoration of madmen.'

The next eight stanzas are very unequal. The poet longs for his vision, the poor for some escape from their distress. The nations together cry to the life force that in the past created great advances in civilisation. The people long for someone to intervene, God as the Holy Spirit in the form of a dove, God as what Freud made him, a father figure, or the spirit of science (a mild engineer). But life replies that there is no exterior force that can solve the people's problems: 'I am whatever you do'. You yourself must choose what is to be. You may build the Just City; you may commit suicide. This is the choice Spain offers.

This part of the argument is awkward and unconvincing. It is not easy to see how the investigator fits the argument and phrases such as 'furious papa', 'the bar-companion', and 'the easily-duped' are too slick. The following three stanzas are much more effective. The images of gulls and seeds evoke a sense of the multitude of people who respond to this challenge and who come from all parts of the world. The verbs 'clung', 'lurch', 'floated' and 'walked' are full of energy and movement. People flock to this centre of crisis, where our sickness may be healed now, or not at all.

The pictures of the future have not this sense of purpose, and often appear unreal, like William Morris's utopian descriptions of London in *News from Nowhere*. We cannot envisage a world without conflict, and the description of the bicycle races, the summer evenings and the walks by the lake are like a dream. But in the final stanza, Auden's theatrical rhetoric at last is completely successful. We can no longer discover meaning in the universe by studying the stars. We are not in tune with Nature, for the animals are unconcerned by our fate. Human beings are alone, and have the power of choice. For the last time in twentieth-century English poetry, a poet offers an heroic myth to his readers. Here you may choose, and if we win, the Just City will arise.

Now the battles in Spain and the succeeding world war are over, the heroic ideal has been almost completely abandoned. Modern poets such as Larkin regard heroic postures with scepticism or suspicion. Ted Hughes and Thom Gunn have little faith in purposeful action. We have seen too much suffering to entertain any longer the old utopian dreams. But who are we to say that Auden was wrong, and that if the leaders of the free nations had made an heroic choice in the Thirties, the future would look so dark as it does today?

II

O DREAMS, O DESTINATIONS

by C. Day Lewis

1

For infants time is like a humming shell
Heard between sleep and sleep, wherein the shores
Foam-fringed, wind-fluted of the strange earth dwell
And the sea's cavernous hunger faintly roars.
It is the humming pole of summer lanes
Whose sound quivers like heat-haze endlessly
Over the corn, over the poppied plains—
An emanation from the earth or sky.
Faintly they hear, through the womb's lingering haze,
A rumour of that sea to which they are born:
They hear the ringing pole of summer days,
But need not know what hungers for the corn.
They are the lisping rushes in a stream—
Grace-notes of a profound, legato dream.

2

Children look down upon the morning-grey
Tissue of mist that veils a valley's lap:
Their fingers itch to tear it and unwrap
The flags, the roundabouts, the gala day.
They watch the spring rise inexhaustibly—
A breathing thread out of the eddied sand,
Sufficient to their day: but half their mind
Is on the sailed and glittering estuary.

Fondly we wish their mist might never break,
Knowing it hides so much that best were hidden:
We'd chain them by the spring, lest it should broaden
For them into a quicksand and a wreck.
But they slip through our fingers like the source,
Like mist, like time that has flagged out their course.

3

That was the fatal move, the ruination
Of innocence so innocently begun,
When in the lawless orchard of creation
The child left this fruit for that rosier one.
Reaching towards the far thing, we begin it;
Looking beyond, or backward, more and more
We grow unfaithful to the unique minute
Till, from neglect, its features stale and blur.
Fish, bird or beast was never thus unfaithful—
Man only casts the image of his joys
Beyond his senses' reach; and by this fateful
Act, he confirms the ambiguous power of choice.
Innocence made that first choice. It is she
Who weeps, a child chained to the outraged tree.

4

Our youthtime passes down a colonnade
Shafted with alternating light and shade.
All's dark or dazzle there. Half in a dream
Rapturously we move, yet half afraid
Never to wake. That diamond-point, extreme
Brilliance engraved on us a classic theme:
The shaft of darkness had its lustre too,
Rising where earth's concentric mysteries gleam.
Oh youth-charmed hours, that made an avenue
Of fountains playing us on to love's full view,

A cypress walk to some romantic grave—
Waking, how false in outline and in hue
We find the dreams that flickered on our cave:
Only your fire, which cast them, still seems true.

5

All that time there was thunder in the air:
Our nerves branched and flickered with summer lightning.
The taut crab-apple, the pampas quivering, the glare
On the roses seemed irrelevant, or a heightening
At most of the sealed-up hour wherein we awaited
What?—some explosive oracle to abash
The platitudes on the lawn? heaven's delegated
Angel—the golden rod, our burning bush?
No storm broke. Yet in retrospect the rose
Mounting vermilion, fading, glowing again
Like a fire's heart, that breathless inspiration
Of pampas grass, crab-tree's attentive pose
Never were so divinely charged as then—
The veiled Word's flesh, a near annunciation.

6

Symbols of gross experience!—our grief
Flowed, like a sacred river, underground:
Desire bred fierce abstractions on the mind,
Then like an eagle soared beyond belief.
Often we tried our breast against the thorn,
Our paces on the turf: whither we flew,
Why we should agonize, we hardly knew—
Nor what ached in us, asking to be born.
Ennui of youth!—thin air above the clouds,
Vain divination of the sunless stream
Mirror that impotence, till we redeem
Our birthright, and the shadowplay concludes.

Ah, not in dreams, but when our souls engage
With the common mesh and moil, we come of age.

7

Older, we build a road where once our active
Heat threw up mountains and the deep dales veined:
We're glad to gain the limited objective,
Knowing the war we fight in has no end.
The road must needs follow each contour moulded
By that fire in its losing fight with earth:
We march over our past, we may behold it
Dreaming a slave's dream on our bivouac hearth.
Lost the archaic dawn wherein we started,
The appetite for wholeness: now we prize
Half-loaves, half-truths—enough for the half-hearted,
The gleam snatched from corruption satisfies.
Dead youth, forgive us if, all but defeated,
We raise a trophy where your honour lies.

8

But look, the old illusion still returns,
Walking a field-path where the succory burns
Like summer's eye, blue lustre-drops of noon,
And the heart follows it and freshly yearns:
Yearns to the sighing distances beyond
Each height of happiness, the vista drowned
In gold-dust haze, and dreams itself immune
From change and night to which all else is bound.
Love, we have caught perfection for a day
As succory holds a gem of halcyon ray:
Summer burns out, its flower will tarnish soon—
Deathless illusion, that could so relay
The truth of flesh and spirit, sun and clay
Singing for once together all in tune!

9

To travel like a bird, lightly to view
Deserts where stone gods founder in the sand,
Ocean embraced in a white sleep with land;
To escape time, always to start anew.
To settle like a bird, make one devoted
Gesture of permanence upon the spray
Of shaken stars and autumns; in a bay
Beyond the crestfallen surges to have floated.
Each is our wish. Alas, the bird flies blind,
Hooded by a dark sense of destination:
Her weight on the glass calm leaves no impression,
Her home is soon a basketful of wind.
Travellers, we're fabric of the road we go;
We settle, but like feathers on time's flow.

'O Dreams, O Destinations' is a sonnet sequence, a poem
made up of nine stanzas, each written in what is generally
thought to be the tightest of traditional forms. There are formid-
able precedents to remember when reading it: love sonnets by
Shakespeare and Sidney, religious sonnets by Donne and
Hopkins, 'nature' sonnets by Wordsworth. Obviously Day
Lewis's sequence is not on the same level of achievement as
these, but the Sonnet Sequence has always been a popular form:
one recalls examples by (among others) D. G. Rossetti, Swinburne, Robert Bridges, Elizabeth Barrett Browning, and Francis
Thompson. In the mid-twentieth century the best sonnet
sequence is very probably Auden's 'In Time of War'. C. Day
Lewis's 'O Dreams, O Destinations' was written at about the
same time as Auden's (they were both published during the
Second World War) and comes very close to being as successful.
It is like Auden's sequence (and unlike most others) in that it is
half discursive, half evocative. The poet reflects on the growth of
his mind from childhood to maturity: in theme, his poem is a

kind of shortened *Prelude*. Perhaps both its strength and its weakness is in the ordinariness of the experiences recorded. He makes no special claim for himself, nor does he suggest (as T. S. Eliot sometimes does) that a poet's mind and experience are essentially different from that of the 'ordinary' man (i.e. the man who is not himself a poet or a creative artist of any kind). His sonnets deal with feelings to which many hearts will return an echo, especially hearts that are paired off with intelligent, sensitive and somewhat disillusioned heads. To say this is not to deny that Day Lewis himself, for all his modesty, has gifts far beyond the ordinary. 'O Dreams, O Destinations' is the kind of poem many of us will feel that we could have written ourselves, if we had the creative gift. We then remember that we have not, and that human experiences, however deeply felt, do not turn into poetry of their own accord.

The sonnets in the sequence are technically very varied. The first is regularly Shakespearean, with the rhyme scheme abab/cdcd/efef/gg. The second is a rather unusual variant of the Miltonic sonnet (abba/abba/cddcee), and uses a certain amount of assonance as well as rhyme. The third is Shakespearean again, the fourth has an unusual scheme (aaba/bbcb/ccdcdc) with the five 'c' rhymes for the ear but not for the eye. The eighth sonnet is also interestingly odd. The rhymes are irregular: aaba/ccbc/ddbddb. In opening the sestet with a pronounced (and closed) couplet the poet gives us the sense of an entirely new beginning —this is a device to obtain urgency and immediacy—but the return of the no less pronounced 'b' rhyme then binds the sestet very closely to the octet, and the more so since the octet rhymes (a, b and c) are themselves inter-linked by near assonance. The ninth and final sonnet is a variant of the Shakespearean form.

The internal organisation of the sonnets is skilful, as a close look at any one of them will show. In the first the mood is languorous, a summer evening's spell. We are even reminded of the Pre-Raphaelites, except that the images are more precise than

Rossetti's or Swinburne's would usually be. This mood is reinforced by the gentle alliteration ('sleep ... sleep ... shores', 'foam-fringed, wind-fluted', 'lisping rushes in a stream', and so on), and also by repetition ('faintly' in line 4, taken up at the opening of the sestet; 'hunger' line 4 and 'hungers' line 12; 'humming pole' and 'ringing pole'; 'humming shell' and 'humming pole'; 'summer lanes' and 'summer days'; 'corn' in lines 7 and 12). The images are pervasive (sleep and dreams, wind and sea, sound and music, corn and harvest) and seem to merge into one another as we listen. The recurring nostalgia is kept at low pressure so that one responds to it as to something sad and necessary. The evocativeness of the imagery has in it the genuine mingling of sharpness and haziness with which childhood memories come back to us in relaxed moods. The 'humming pole' is, of course, the telegraph pole carrying wires through the quiet countryside. (I can myself remember being enchanted by this particular magic as a child, somewhere in the heart of Worcestershire: and there is a marvellous use of these humming poles in the Indian film, *Pather Panchali*, which stays in the mind).

In thought, the sonnet sequence passes through the first four of the ages of man. Stanza 1. is about 'infants', stanzas 2 and 3 are about 'children', stanzas 4, 5 and 6 about 'youthtime', stanzas 7, 8 and 9 about being 'older'. In stanza 1, the child's summer contentment is remembered, where even the muted menace of the sea turns into enchantment. Because the infant has no sense of transience, he is near to being immortal. (For the treatment of this theme in an even finer poem, and a different mode, it is worth comparing this with 'Fern Hill'). In stanza 2 the infants become 'children', and the imagery of the first four lines very beautifully captures the eagerness and expectancy of childhood: the certainty that life will turn as the mists clear, into a beautiful summer day. But in both of these sonnets we hear the adult who watches, not the children who hope. Whereas Dylan Thomas *recreates* a child's consciousness in the opening stanzas of 'Fern

Hill', Day Lewis recollects and reflects upon it. His recollection is coloured by nostalgia and irony: the paradise is far in the past, guarded by angels with swords. Already there have been ominous if subdued forebodings: the infants in stanza 1 'need not know what hungers for the corn'; the children in stanza 2 are cut off from the adult anxieties to which the sestet is, however, given over. In stanza 3 the adult's knowledge is expressed through symbolism with more explicit reference to a lost Paradise. The fall is interpreted as that 'reaching towards the far thing' which rejects the present for the future: the child descends into mortality as he reaches out. Underlying this is the thought that all true joy lies in the world of the senses. Our intellectual aspiration to something higher than this is itself the original betrayal. In hearkening to it we lose the bliss of the 'unique minute' which even 'fish, bird and beast' enjoy.[1]

[1] It is interesting to compare with this the second stanza in Auden's 'In Time of War':

> They wondered why the fruit had been forbidden;
> It taught them nothing new. They hid their pride,
> But did not listen much when they were chidden;
> They knew exactly what to do outside.

> They left: immediately the memory faded
> Of all they'd learnt; they could not understand
> The dogs now who, before, had always aided;
> The stream was dumb with whom they'd always planned.

> They wept and quarrelled: freedom was so wild.
> In front, maturity, as he ascended,
> Retired like a horizon from the child;

> The dangers and the punishments grew greater;
> And the way back by angels was defended
> Against the poet and the legislator.

This is one of Auden's recurring themes, as poems like 'Our Bias' and 'Time Will Say Nothing But I Told You So' also show: the moment when men depart from their momentary perfection, and lose by reflection the fullness which even animals and plants attain.

For a powerful contrast with Day Lewis's feeling one might compare Yeats's 'Sailing to Byzantium'—surely one of the greatest modern poems in which the claims of sensuality and intellect are weighed against one another.

Nevertheless, there are compensations. Youth may have lost Paradise, but it knows love. In sonnet 4 the heightened vicissitudes of young love are beautifully captured in the octet, though the voice of middle age returns in the sestet, to comment sadly on this second illusion. The turning of the expected 'grove' into 'grave' in line 11 (a transmutation reinforced by the fact that it is a rhyming word) is a device to remind us of Dylan Thomas. In the closing line the reference to the Platonic cave once again dismisses any hope of ideal realities 'beyond the senses' reach'.

Stanza 5 concentrates on one particular aspect of youthful hope: those rare but splendid moments when we seem on the very verge of breaking through to some greater understanding and fulfilment. Such moments are the nearest approach to mystical experience that most of us make. They recall Wordsworth's spots of time—with the important difference, however, that whereas Wordsworth believed in their transcendental validity, Day Lewis very clearly does not.

The sixth sonnet moves us on to the no-man's-land of late youth: to full engagement, at last, with life's 'common mesh and moil', when dreams and enchantments fade, almost for ever. Wordsworth, of course, believed that this is exactly what did not happen to a poet. The majority of men might journey into the 'light of common day', but the poet is precisely the man who keeps his sense of wonder, his creative imagination, alive. For Day Lewis the awakening into daylight is inevitable, and the highest hopes of childhood and youth are indeed mere dreams. Perhaps this is why we feel the whole sequence as a kind of intimation of mortality from recollections of earliest middle-age; why for all its charm and accomplishment we do not respond, in the end, as we do to major verse.

Stanza 7 expresses, only too well, the world of 'half-loaves, half-truths' which most of us in fact inhabit, whether we like it or not; a world in which well-intentioned liberalism is carefully balanced against expediency; where we cry, from the midst of comparative wealth and respectability, that 'we're glad to gain the limited objective', but alas!—that our appetite for wholeness has somehow gone.

There is nothing in stanza 8 to modify this. For brief periods the 'old illusion still returns', and now the poet celebrates it without disillusioning comment—except that he calls it illusion, and his very rhythms suggest a tiredness born of this word. Stanza 9, one of the most beautiful, closes the poem with a bird's-eye view, in which the poet's agnosticism achieves a full and rounded expression.

In running through the theme of 'O Dreams, O Destinations', judgements have necessarily been implied. One could scarcely read the poem without judging at every point—but may it not be one of Day Lewis's faults that we do? The greatest poems do not argue, they create: we enter into Wordsworth's experiences in *The Prelude* or T. S. Eliot's in *Four Quartets*, and the philosophical problem 'Do I agree?' is an irrelevance. In this poem the question 'Do I agree?' pursues us throughout. The symbols are charming and evocative, but they are not irrefutable; they are even tendentious, in that they evoke one particular interpretation of human experiences (a very common one admittedly), along with the experiences themselves. When we look closer, perhaps we are not wholly sure where the poet himself stands. Is he lamenting life's inevitable disenchantments, as he sees them to be? Or is he at some level accusing himself for his own lament, for his betrayal of the 'dead youth' whom his manhood has outraged? The irony of the title could be taken either way. There is no full-blooded wisdom of acceptance just as there is no full-blooded anger of protest. The mood of the poem is depressed; and this depression slightly infects the creative vitality, for all its excellence.

It may be that the greatest poetry needs energy if not belief and that Day Lewis is dealing with exactly the kind of response to life that saps such energy. Yet to say this without qualification would be to end on a distorted note. This sonnet sequence is one that can be returned to with pleasure: it is a splendidly civilised poem.

12

POEM FOR ELSA *by Michael Roberts*

THAT day the blue-black rook fell pitifully dead
You wept and stormed, tossing your lovely head,
Hurling commiseration into broken skies
That wept and wept, vainly as any eyes.

You pitifully wept, nor would be comforted
Till a bedraggled robin chirped unfed
Begging for comfort-crumbs, and sought your aid
To mend a world you had not made.

You who compassionately wept, be with me still,
Though the wind lash the dark, the wooded hill;
The hand that let the wild wet creature ache
Moulded the heart that grieves, but shall not break.

This is a 'simple' poem in a double sense; it is easy to understand, and there is no tension of contraries in the mood. The
movement is lyrical and tender. Michael Roberts's talent is of
that civilised and sensitive kind which has produced much of the
very best minor verse in all ages: often 'minor' seems too grudging a word, as it does if applied, without qualification, to the
poem before us now. The fact is that Michael Roberts is much
less well known to present-day readers than he ought to be,
partly through his own modesty when editing *The Faber Book
Of Modern Verse*. He left himself out of it, for reasons one can
respect but also regret. Though he is not as good a poet as Auden
and MacNeice, and not as good most of the time as Spender,
it is very possible to think of him in the same general terms as

C. Day Lewis. He is arguably a finer poet, in many essential respects, than certain better-known figures like George Barker. His *Collected Poems* is now available, and is a volume that most poetry lovers will want to possess and return to from time to time.

The poem's theme, as I have said, is very simple. Elsa is a little girl weeping over a dead rook. The poet is recalling this episode later in his life, as a moment still vividly present to him. The child was touched by the sight of the dead bird, and grieved inconsolably. She was comforted only when a living bird—a robin—appeared on the scene, in need of help. Then she was able to *give* to it: not as much help as her pity for the rook appeared to demand, but enough to open the path to 'comfort'. In the last stanza, the poet returns to the present, and asks Elsa to be with him in his own time of grief. She may be alive but absent; she may be dead, and present only in the poet's memory. It is even possible that it is her own death he is writing about, and that her childish pity for a dead rook remains for him, in his darkness, as a healing thought.

That is what the poem is about, and there is nothing in the mood to qualify it. There is, however, a depth of reference which the casual reader might miss. The mood of the poem is sombre, but not defeated. Like many poets of the 1930's Michael Roberts was deeply concerned about the plight of the world, and haunted by a sense of doom. A great many of his poems record the encroaching darkness of the time, as Europe's lights went out one by one. In social terms, he was less optimistic than Auden and Spender; he saw little comfort, it seems, for the human race. But unlike most of his contemporaries he was a Christian: the sorrows he recorded were often personal (as here), even when a political theme was his first concern. His Christianity was far removed from dogma or exuberance. It alleviated rather than banished the pessimism to which he was naturally prone. Perhaps it can best be described as an undercurrent of compassionate attention to suffering (which we also find in many non-Christian poets, of course), leading to religious hope of a curiously muted kind.

'Poem to Elsa' is about compassion; a little girl's tears for a bird. We are made conscious of the twin aspects of compassion that may present themselves at moments of grief: its practical uselessness (the rook remains dead, and well beyond the reach of tears), and its intrinsic worth: useful or not, it is the most human response that can be made. The criterion of 'usefulness' is important, but the meaning of compassion is not wholly to be discussed in its terms. Elsa's tears for the dead rook do not bring it to life again, but they do lead on to kindness to the robin. The community between man and beast is kept open by them—as, too, is the community between man and man, and possibly (the last stanza suggests) the community between man and God. We are made to feel that the child's response, far from being 'sentimental' (how often are sneers at 'sentimentality' an unacknowledged defence of callousness?) is deeply human; that it has power over life, even if death is beyond its writ. Inevitably we are reminded of the words of Christ, 'Are not two sparrows sold for a farthing? and one of them shall not fall on the ground without your Father'. There can be little doubt that Christ's words reach out as far as religious (and human) hope can go—though not further than hope feels it must go, in certain moments of strain. Tennyson's *In Memoriam* is as striking an expression as we have of the wish that even the humblest and most transient creatures might have some final purpose, to justify their lives:

> That nothing walks with aimless feet;
>   That not one life shall be destroy'd,
>   Or cast as rubbish to the void,
> When God hath made the pile complete;
>
> That not a worm is cloven in vain;
>   That not a moth with vain desire
>   Is shrivel'd in a fruitless fire,
> Or but subserves another's gain.

Tennyson wrote under the double stress of bereavement and doubt; the poem we are considering now is less agonised than *In Memoriam* but it occupies the same area of wishes and fears. It does not ask questions as *In Memoriam* does, but it does suggest hope, through the very questions that might be asked. The child's grief did not bring the rook back to life, but it helped the robin. We are reminded that if there is any hope of a divine compassion for creation, then human compassion is as near an approach to it as we are likely to make. In the last stanza the poet's grief is itself moved towards religious hope by the recollection of this:

> The hand that let the wild wet creature ache
> Moulded the heart that grieves, but shall not break.

Is 'the wild wet creature' Elsa, or the rook? This is the one point where the poet is deliberately ambiguous, but on either interpretation, and it appears that the two are meant to be seen as the same, we are made to feel pity as a healing and cleansing power.

The poem's form is as simple as its theme. Each stanza consists of two couplets; all of the lines except one (line 8) can just about be scanned as iambic pentameters, though line 3 resists very toughly, and the attempt to scan merely reveals how far away the poet's voice is from a metrical norm. The tone is conversational and grave, holding sentimentality well within the bounds of a true compassion. Much depends upon the delicate repetition of key words and phrases, 'wept and stormed', 'wept and wept', 'pitifully wept', and 'compassionately wept'. The lyric is subdued in its music; the intensity comes straight from the theme itself. It is the kind of poem that one can truly call an education in human feeling, even though there is no overt moral of any kind.

There is a final matter which the poem forces upon our attention, and that is the 'pathetic fallacy', as Ruskin called it. What Ruskin meant by this was the kind of poetic usage which ascribes human feelings to inanimate objects, colouring land-scapes and living creatures with human motives and moods. In defining the pathetic fallacy, Ruskin had his own axe to grind. He was very concerned to establish 'Nature' (the external world) as an objective reality in its own right; he wanted us to learn to 'see' Nature as it really is, and this kind of 'seeing' was interfered with, he thought, by the various moods, wishes, fears, stock responses and so on which we are apt to project upon the world round about us.

The pathetic fallacy is too large a subject to enter into at length, but a modern reader will obviously treat it with the greatest reserve. In parts of his essay, Ruskin is merely urging that flowers and waves do not *really* have the emotions poets ascribe to them, and with this we should no doubt agree. But at other times he seems to suggest that all metaphors are lies unless they are written out as similes—and this surely overlooks the essential nature of language, as well as implying a distinctly unflattering opinion of the intelligence of most of the readers a poet will have.

The manner in which man and Nature (i.e. the world outside man) interact is very complex, as any modern philosopher or psychologist would admit. There are many ways in which we can respond to Nature, many ways in which we can interpret it, many ways in which we can use it for the purposes of art. When a Platonist or a mystic talks of Nature's 'life' he refers to a real quality, perceived supersensuously by himself. When Words-worth or Coleridge talk of it, they mean partly this, and partly something else: the 'life' is to some extent given by their own creative energy, a creation of the God *within* the mind. Many further possibilities could be adduced. Dickens's novels are full of descriptions of streets, houses, ships and so on, imbued with distinctive and even eccentric human qualities, but this time there is no mystical suggestiveness: what we are conscious of is a richness of fancy turning, under the pressure of the novel as a whole, into symbolism. This, in turn, reminds us that many great writers use symbolism more or less consciously, and that such thematic images as the fog in *Bleak House* or *The Waste Land*, the water in *The Mill On The Floss* and *Romola*, the heath and moorland in *The Return Of The Native* and *Wuthering Heights* have a far profounder relationship to human destiny than the simple colouring of Nature by our moods or whims can even begin to explain.

The objection to Ruskin's 'pathetic fallacy' is that it is a blunt critical implement; it overlooks the diversity of creative usage, and begs far more questions than it solves. Sometimes it becomes an almost routine offensive weapon against poets or poems a critic does not happen to like. 'Poem For Elsa' is exactly a poem where we have to be on our guard. The idea of 'broken skies', weeping as if in sympathy with the child, looks like a pathetic fallacy; so does the idea of the robin 'begging' and seeking for aid. Skies, Ruskin would insist, do not weep; robins do not beg; therefore the poet is either being feeble-minded, or he is telling lies. Nevertheless, poets always will use metaphors, and readers always will distinguish without too much difficulty between objective 'fact' and the emotional colouring that facts are made to bear.

'Poem For Elsa' is a statement about human emotions, and as such, it is simply true. Our strong moods of joy or sorrow do spread a colouring over the external world. The rook's death occurred on a rainy day, and the sympathy between man and Nature is such that a link between the two must inevitably be formed. It would, indeed, be impossible for a human mind not to be affected by the external world, and perhaps especially by the weather, in moments of grief. Our mind works through the association of similar ideas under the colour of emotion. This record of a grief which merges with the rain outside has the force of simple reporting, in addition to such further religious significances as there are.

The robin, on the other hand, is not sentimentalised at all. He comes to be fed, and though 'begging' is a human word, it is probably the nearest and least misleading we could find. It expresses the poet's sense of a 'filial bond' between man and Nature, which many poets have believed to be of the highest reality and truth. The fact that a vulture's dealings with man may be different from a robin's is not in question; nor is the fact that a robin could not be expected to respond to the help it 'begs' with gratitude, or hatred, as a human might. Anyone who has ever fed birds will know perfectly well what the poet means, without imagining that he has confused the robin with a man. Anyone again, who has responded to the created world with sympathy or love will know that Elsa's feelings for the rook and the robin are not weak-minded. They are, as the poet enforces, worthy of our deepest respect.

These points are worth making, since though obvious, they are very likely to be overlooked. A great deal of lyrical poetry is undervalued by critics who hold Ruskin's view, or who hold (as is more probable) some simplified corruption of it. 'Poem For Elsa' lends itself to an easy dismissal from such critics; but one hopes that most readers will not be tempted in this way.

13

VANITY *by Robert Graves*

BE assured, the Dragon is not dead
But once more from the pools of peace
Shall rear his fabulous green head.

The flowers of innocence shall cease
And like a harp the wind shall roar
And the clouds shake an angry fleece.

'Here, here is certitude,' you swore,
'Below this lightning-blasted tree.
Where once it strikes, it strikes no more.

'Two lovers in one house agree.
The roof is tight, the walls unshaken.
As now, so must it always be.'

Such prophecies of joy awaken
The toad who dreams away the past
Under your hearth-stone, light forsaken,

Who knows that certitude at last
Must melt away in vanity—
No gate is fast, no door is fast—

That thunder bursts from the blue sky,
That gardens of the mind fall waste,
That fountains of the heart run dry.

The opening of the poem might be described as a Bardic
Imperative. Graves is a poet who enjoys dressing common sense

in a richly embroidered garb. 'Be assured . . .', 'Here, here is certitude . . .', 'Who knows . . .'. There is a largeness of gesture here, to remind us of a host of mid-eighteenth-century poets in bardic mood. This comparison can be pushed a little further. The tone of many of Graves's poems reminds us of the mid-eighteenth century—in stylistic conventions which suggest that civilised commonplaces have become, all at once, insights of a uniquely prophetic kind; in a manner which is at once *de haut en bas* and yet still on terms of equality with its readers. The disabling feature of mid-eighteenth-century verse was a frequent loss of belief in itself, which collapsed the elaborate pretensions into a game. But Graves is free from this fault. His belief in his own poetry is always complete, like his belief in the ideas he writes about. The very lack of humour is sometimes felt as a positive quality, if of a somewhat stifling kind. Above all, perhaps, he sees no war as the eighteenth-century writers sometimes did between the idea of the poet as maker (the Greek *poiein*) and poet as prophet (the Roman *vates*). Sometimes, poets and their critics have felt these two possibilities as alternatives, the one leading to a purely technical view of poetry, the other to a purely inspirational one. But Graves thinks of himself as both craftsman and prophet: Apollo and the White Goddess are reconciled in his verse.

Reading 'Vanity' for the first time our attention will first be given to the dragon. Is it symbolic, and if so, what does it symbolise? The answer is symbolic, yes, but not primarily so. One of the great traps in critical analysis is to seize on a poem's symbols, especially when they are as tempting as this, and to translate them into abstractions. The analysing intellect falls on its prey before our visual imagination has had any sort of a chance. Even the greatest of poets have not escaped this fate, for reasons one can sympathise with, if not approve. One agrees that it is useful to know what a poem 'means'; it is useful to know that Shakespeare, for example, thought good better than evil, love better than hate. But at the same time, if we are *literary* critics, we want to know a great deal more. Great poetry is not simply a translation of platitudes into riddles, nor is criticism a retranslation of riddles back into platitudes again. When approaching a poem, it may even be necessary to hold our analysing intellect in check, until we have first visualised and heard; until our imagination has been captured as if by a revelation. The poem comes to us from outside, and only when we have received it on its own terms can any fruitful dialogue between ourselves and it begin. This dialogue depends, of course, on the range and depth of our own literary experience, against which the new poem will sooner or later have to stand. It does, however, presuppose the secondary rôle of the analysing intellect in critical appreciation, since we have to guard against diminishing poems to our own previous experience of life, when we should be enlarging ourselves in the ways they might suggest.

In this poem, our first work is to visualise the dragon before we generalise it, to establish it as a real dragon, with the right mingling of wonder and fear. Fortunately, Graves makes this easy, since the first stanza is one of the most arresting images in modern verse. The whole vocabulary is exotic ('pools of peace', 'fabulous green head') and there is both fascination and terror in the thought of this submerged menace waiting to rise. The 'reality' of the dragon is part social, part personal to every individual who reads. It comes from childhood fears, from fairy tales, from nightmares, from medieval romances, from *Paradise Lost* (where the 'toad' also has a place), from myths and tales of various kinds, Loch Ness most of all. A psychologist might try to *explain* the manner in which our fears and insecurities embody themselves in such images; a poet's work is to *achieve* such embodiment, as Graves very powerfully does here. The poem's 'meaning' depends on our full response to the dragon—without which its intellectual bones would seem skeletal, and its somewhat eerie pessimism would be lost.

In stanza 2 the ravages of the awakened dragon turn into other images, simple, traditional and somewhat austere. The flowers are age-old emblems, the harp is one of the great bardic (and romantic) images of inspiration. There is an almost dream-like vision of life translated into death: Graves does not explain why this is, but simply offers pictures, like rapid transitions in a nightmare. (It is interesting to compare his technique here with Blake's 'Chapel in the Green', where the same kind of visualisation of fantastic symbols is required before the poem can be 'understood'.)

The third and fourth stanzas bring this imagery to bear upon the poem's main theme, which is the decay of love. The tone becomes conversational—it is the dialogue of many lovers at the moment of certitude—and the lovers' simple assurance is set in this atmosphere of cosmic foreboding. Sitting beside the pools of peace, they have forgotten the dragon. The poet's own vantage point is that of the opening 'Be assured', from which the mood of grimly prophetic foreboding is derived.

In stanza 5 the dragon is replaced, symbolically, by the toad, equally menacing, but more sordid and squat. We are bound to recall the moment in Book IV of *Paradise Lost* when Satan is found 'Squat like a Toad, close at the ear of Eve', whispering evil infections into her dreams. The toad becomes a sinister embodiment of the poem's main burden,

> that certitude at last
> Must melt away in vanity—

Why?—because human 'prophecies of joy' awaken an ancient and implacable envy in the universe, which will always destroy them.

We can see now exactly why the dragon and the toad must be visually and imaginatively real to us before we respond to them as symbols. The poet is deliberately not letting us know what they 'arc', in any sense of simple allegory that can be translated.

In this sense, they may be some flaw in the human heart, a kind of original sin; they may be some flaw in the universe, a cosmic hostility or indifference to man; they may be transience itself, the inexorable law to which all men are bound. The strength of the poem is that though these and possibly other interpretations are bound to occur to us, the poet is not concerned with them simply as theories. His concern is to remind us of the menace surrounding human life, of the dragon sleeping but not dead beneath the pools of peace, of the toad 'who dreams away the past Under your hearth-stone, light forsaken...'. The tone of the poem—incantatory, insistent, deliberately monotonous despite the colourful imagery and the prophesies of storm—relates to these images. The final images of transience in the last stanza are again austerely unembroidered, but the remembrance of the dragon and the toad establishes the menace as living, and therefore malevolent, rather than as simply some impersonal force.

The poem's theme is a classic example of the kind of common sense in which prophets deal. Graves is saying nothing new, but he offers the old with a sombre intensity. In the word 'vanity' itself, there is a reference to the Wisdom tradition of the Old Testament. Clearly Graves is not using the word in its modern sense, but in the same way as Ecclesiastes, 'Vanity of vanities, saith the Preacher, vanity of vanities; all is vanity. What profit hath a man of all his labour which he taketh under the sun? One generation passeth away, and another generation cometh: but the earth abideth for ever.' 'Vanity' is exactly the preacher's word to describe all human activities, love as well as hate, achievement as well as failure, in the light of eternity.

But though Graves uses a favourite word of the Wisdom writers, he lacks their patience. One can feel the sharp tang of bitterness in the poem, which is half tough recognition and proclamation, half brooding fierceness and anger. The tone is nearer to protest than Wisdom writing would be, though there is no one to whom the protest can be addressed. The vision is a grim one, of sin without redemption, whether in man's heart or in the cosmos itself. The poem enforces itself on us almost as a celebration of the dragon and the toad. At least they are more eternal than man, more assured of their final triumph over his paltry certitudes. It is an arid triumph, as the final images suggest.

Perhaps one feels something slightly vicarious, looking back, in that 'Be assured', as if the poet is identifying himself with this grimness. It is hard to think of this poem as the equal of Blake's technically similar 'Chapel in the Green' despite its imaginative richness, and its arresting theme.

14

FERN HILL *by Dylan Thomas*

Now as I was young and easy under the apple boughs
About the lilting house and happy as the grass was green,
   The night above the dingle starry,
    Time let me hail and climb
   Golden in the heydays of his eyes,
And honoured among wagons I was prince of the apple towns
And once below a time I lordly had the trees and leaves
    Trail with daisies and barley
   Down the rivers of the windfall light.

And as I was green and carefree, famous among the barns
About the happy yard and singing as the farm was home,
   In the sun that is young once only,
    Time let me play and be
   Golden in the mercy of his means,
And green and golden I was huntsman and herdsman, the calves
Sang to my horn, the foxes on the hills barked clear and cold,
    And the sabbath rang slowly
   In the pebbles of the holy streams.

All the sun long it was running, it was lovely, the hay
Fields high as the house, the tunes from the chimneys, it was air
   And playing, lovely and watery
    And fire green as grass.
   And nightly under the simple stars
As I rode to sleep the owls were bearing the farm away,

All the moon long I heard, blessed among stables, the night-jars
　Flying with the ricks, and the horses
　　Flashing into the dark.

And then to awake, and the farm, like a wanderer white
With the dew, come back, the cock on his shoulder: it was all
　Shining, it was Adam and maiden,
　　The sky gathered again
　And the sun grew round that very day.
So it must have been after the birth of the simple light
In the first, spinning place, the spellbound horses walking warm
　Out of the whinnying green stable
　　On to the fields of praise.

And honoured among foxes and pheasants by the gay house
Under the new made clouds and happy as the heart was long,
　In the sun born over and over,
　　I ran my heedless ways,
　My wishes raced through the house high hay
And nothing I cared, at my sky blue trades, that time allows
In all his tuneful turning so few and such morning songs
　Before the children green and golden
　　Follow him out of grace,

Nothing I cared, in the lamb white days, that time would take me
Up to the swallow thronged loft by the shadow of my hand,
　In the moon that is always rising,
　　Nor that riding to sleep
　I should hear him fly with the high fields
And wake to the farm forever fled from the childless land.
Oh as I was young and easy in the mercy of his means,
　　Time held me green and dying
　Though I sang in my chains like the sea.

'Fern Hill' is deservedly one of the most popular of Dylan
Thomas's poems. Wonderfully rich and full of vitality, the words

combine together in highly original ways to picture the joyful exhilaration of a child. This originality confuses some readers. Striking phrases such as 'happy as the grass was green', 'prince of the apple towns', or 'at my sky blue trades', surprise by their novelty, and at first it is difficult to be sure what effects are intended. These unusual images are evocative rather than precise; and their purpose is to create a strong emotional response, rather than to define a particular attitude. Thomas deliberately uses all his wit and subtlety to gather into each image a wide range of associations. Essentially a romantic poet, he is trying to communicate an experience which is almost beyond expression. In the repetitions 'it was lovely', 'it was air And playing, lovely and watery . . .', he seems to be straining after an ecstasy which can never be wholly confined into words.

This type of poetry has often been held in low esteem by modern analytic critics, who have little to say about the large emotional effects achieved through evocative rhythms and imagery. It is true that some of the images in 'Fern Hill' appear to have been chosen at random; for example, what effects are intended by the line: 'Down the rivers of the windfall light'? And other similar examples make the poem as a whole a little diffuse; but there is no point in over-emphasising this. Thomas is celebrating the divine innocence of a child, and for him this is a mystery beyond analysis.

The magical landscapes of the poem have a twofold effect. They create anew the freshness and wonder of a child's vision, but at the same time they express Thomas's adult interpretation of his past experience. This is not forced upon the reader by direct comment or moralising, but is shown in and through the concrete pictures of the boy's life on the farm. A good example of this occurs at the end of the second stanza.

> And the sabbath rang slowly
> In the pebbles of the holy streams.

These lines remind us how for a child roaming the countryside, time moves slowly through long mornings of pleasure. But much more than this is implied. The noise of water passing over the pebbles is like church bells calling the boy to worship. Thomas conveys his adult belief that the boy's awakening to the beauty of Nature has a divine significance, and that all human joy is holy.

A comparable example can be seen in the middle of the third stanza. After a day of excitement the child, as he falls to sleep, continues to feel the movements of the day—'as I rode to sleep'. But the continuation of movement into the night, as the boy hears the owls and nightjars, suggests a mysterious and unending vitality in Nature itself. In the phrases 'under the simple stars' and 'blessed among stables', the words 'simple' and 'blessed' are introduced not to make explicit a definite religious viewpoint, but to evoke a general feeling of reverence for the innocence of a child.

The gaiety and strength of the poem come largely from this type of adult interpretation. Thomas is aware of the power of time, but, instead of becoming melancholy and nostalgic, he sees the joy of his childhood as something for which to be thankful, and as itself part of the wonder of all creation; instead of giving way to regrets, he exults in what has been. The boy does not appear in any way separate from his surroundings. This effect is achieved in part by the use of transferred epithets—"the lilting house', 'happy yard', 'gay house'. These words describe how the boy's emotions transform every object he perceives; but also they prevent us from feeling that he lives in an alien environment. The boy is 'honoured among foxes and pheasants by the gay house'—an integral part of all created things.

For Thomas the child achieves an exalted state, for he is a 'prince', 'honoured' and 'lordly', a rightful inheritor of the blessings of Nature. Lines such as 'the hay fields high as the house' evoke a sense of abundance, of a world of plenty of which the boy's exuberance is but a part. He is 'green and golden', innocent and yet overheaped with gifts. His mind moves rapidly from one impression to the next; and this energy is reflected in the many quick movements of the poem—'All the sun long it was running . . .', where the lilting rhythm, with its light stresses—'happy as the grass was green'—carries the reader on in quick surges of delight. The long sentences, beautifully constructed and controlled by Thomas, give this feeling of continuous pleasure; no sharp breaks interrupt the exuberant flow.

These expressions of mystery and power move to a climax in stanza four. When the boy awakes in the morning, the farm appears like the Garden of Eden, a revelation of innocence. It is typical of Thomas that this new awareness is expressed in concrete terms. When dealing with comparable experiences, Wordsworth moves away from the actual towards a mysticism beyond the world of the senses. He talks of 'something far more deeply interfused' in Nature, and tries to find expression for an awareness of the transcendental—'The winds come to me from the fields of sleep.' Thomas's sense of wonder comes from participation in life itself, for he glories in what is revealed through the senses, and does not look beyond. The spellbound horses are mysterious, to be praised in song, not as symbols of a transcendental reality, but for their own force and beauty.

From the beginning of the poem, the child's simple unreflecting vitality is seen as a gift of time, soon to be withdrawn. These references to time have a double effect. The words 'all the sun long', 'all the moon long', show how the child measured time by light, not by the clock, and how each day seems a long savouring of experience; but they also remind us that this experience is not permanent. In the final two stanzas, the facts of time become more insistent, and the pathos of transience can no longer be ignored. Yet even in these concluding lines, no suggestion is given that the child's experience is in any way inadequate. 'Nothing I cared' is a simple statement of fact, not a moral comment on the heedlessness of the child. Time may hold the child 'green and dying', but he sings in his chains; he is 'like the sea', full of abundance and infinite power.

The effect of the last line is essentially imprecise, and its success comes largely from the music of the poem. Thomas was a constant experimenter in verse, and always used words deliberately for musical effects. The quality of this poem comes largely from a careful use of ecstatic rhythms; in the last lines, we have a last flourish of rhythmic exaltation, with the image of the sea gathering together into itself all the previous evocations of heroism and abundance.

In the literature of the post-1945 world, so often full of anger and despair, Thomas's faith in life seems to some people naïve. But in this poem time and death are accepted as undeniable facts, yet Thomas's attitude is one of courage and sanity. In a world faced by total destruction, he reminds us of the wonder and mystery of individual experience, and for this we ourselves should be thankful.

15

THE HORSES *by Edwin Muir*

BARELY a twelvemonth after
The seven days war that put the world to sleep,
Late in the evening the strange horses came.
By then we had made our covenant with silence,
But in the first few days it was so still
We listened to our breathing and were afraid.
On the second day
The radios failed; we turned the knobs; no answer.
On the third day a warship passed us, heading north,
Dead bodies piled on the deck. On the sixth day
A plane plunged over us into the sea. Thereafter
Nothing. The radios dumb;
And still they stand in corners of our kitchens,
And stand, perhaps, turned on, in a million rooms
All over the world. But now if they should speak,
If on a sudden they should speak again,
If on the stroke of noon a voice should speak,
We would not listen, we would not let it bring
The old bad world that swallowed its children quick
At one great gulp. We would not have it again.
Sometimes we think of the nations lying asleep,
Curled blindly in impenetrable sorrow,
And then the thought confounds us with its strangeness.

The tractors lie about our fields; at evening
They look like dank sea-monsters couched and waiting.
We leave them where they are and let them rust:

'They'll moulder away and be like other loam'.
We make our oxen drag our rusty ploughs,
Long laid aside. We have gone back
Far past our fathers' land.

       And then, that evening
Late in the summer the strange horses came.
We heard a distant tapping on the road,
A deepening drumming; it stopped, went on again
And at the corner changed to hollow thunder.
We saw the heads
Like a wild wave charging and were afraid.
We had sold our horses in our fathers' time
To buy new tractors. Now they were strange to us
As fabulous steeds set on an ancient shield
Or illustrations in a book of knights.
We did not dare go near them. Yet they waited,
Stubborn and shy, as if they had been sent
By an old command to find our whereabouts
And that long-lost archaic companionship.
In the first moment we had never a thought
That they were creatures to be owned and used.
Among them were some half-a-dozen colts
Dropped in some wilderness of the broken world,
Yet new as if they had come from their own Eden.
Since then they have pulled our ploughs and borne our loads,
But that free servitude still can pierce our hearts.
Our life is changed; their coming our beginning.

The search for knowledge has often been thought of as a form
of evil pride. Man's distrust of modern science is embodied in
the stories of Faustus and Frankenstein, and in much popular
reaction to the atom bomb. The first part of this poem reminds us
of the older myths. By his inventions, his radios and warships,

tractors and planes, man has sacrificed himself to a mechanical world, and lost touch with his true nature. The result is a terrifying apocalypse. Muir's purpose is to describe a return to the lost Eden, a re-establishment of the old covenant with God. The seven days war, which turns all to chaos, parodies God's creation of the world in seven days. Afterwards a simpler way of life is restored, with oxen and ploughs, until at last the horses can return to offer their 'long-lost archaic companionship'. The bond between man and Nature is restored.

This is a simple poem, with no complicated imagery, but it achieves a unique and disturbing strangeness. Its form is that of a straightforward story about the future, something rather like a fable, but the sequence of events expresses an extraordinary sense of wonder. Instead of a mere fanciful Arcadian dream, we have a depiction of a state of religious contentment which Christians might accomplish in the present time.

The poem's mixture of simplicity and strangeness is difficult to define. The first three lines contain one sentence, with the main verb placed at the very end, and so given great emphasis. The word 'came' puts the whole story firmly in the past. From the beginning, the tone of the narrative suggest that the experience, however frightening at the time, is now completely accepted. 'Came' is a simple word, as if the arrival of the horses solved all problems in an ordinary way. This 'tone', established in the first sentence, is maintained throughout the poem, and is the real source of its unique simplicity. The sentences are usually long, and the rhythm at times almost like that of a dignified prose narrative. There are no rhymes. The tone is like that of a story-teller recounting his experiences to a group of listeners about a fire-side. The loose structure makes him seem relaxed, looking back in peace at the incredible events of the past. He is not isolated, but speaks for his group. 'We' underwent this conversation, and as a community were reborn into Eden.

The narrator speaks of these miraculous events with awe, and each detail is carefully selected to suggest that these happenings go beyond the ordinary ranges of experience. We are never told what country this is, and all we know of the real landscape is that it is by the sea. The events are unlocalised, and we do not know how many survivors there are. We have left normal reality for the world of fable. Many of the narrator's phrases contain hints of Biblical phraseology. The repetition of 'on a second day', 'the third day', 'the sixth day', recalls Genesis, and words like 'covenant' or 'borne our loads', link the experience of rebirth to the New Testament. The people are going back, far back, to the sources of life.

After the first three lines, the poem quickly establishes the unique quality of the new Eden. The description of a silence 'so still we listened to our breathing and were afraid' takes us from the real world, with its multitude of noises, into a stilled landscape, like some formal medieval painting, or 'illustrations in a book of knights'. The landscape and the events are symbolic, depicting a rebirth into innocence. The disasters of the war contribute to this feeling of strangeness. Who is attending to the engines of the warship, with dead bodies piled on the deck? Where has the plane come from? And the silence of the radios suggests that a whole way of communication has been cut off, that the voices of the old, bad society no longer speak to these people. The tractors become like fabulous sea-monsters, part of an evil world no longer to be tolerated. So the people are prepared for the coming of the divine horses. A distant tapping turns to a drumming and then to a thunder. These approaching noises evoke a growing sense of fear, as if some force is about to erupt which will break their lives. Then there is a short line, which emphasises the heads of the horses, so that we are reminded of tossing manes and glaring eyes. They come like a wild wave as if to destroy all the land. But God speaks in the thunder, and the wave is part of the sea of life. Thunder and wave suggest the power of this new experience, both frightening and exhilarating as it breaks up old habits of thought. So we are reborn into the world of fable, and to a natural relationship with God's creation. Even in our fallen world, a new-born colt has a curious innocence and grace, and this image depicts the new awareness achieved by the people.

The behaviour of the horses exemplifies the new way of life. They are stubborn, determined to have their way, and yet also humble. They have come freely to serve, to bear our loads, and at the end we are reminded of Christ, whose sacrifice still can pierce our hearts. The first movement of the poem ends with the nations asleep, curled like an unborn child in blindness and impenetrable sorrow. The end of the poem is rebirth, a rediscovery of the truth that 'in His service is perfect freedom'.

16

A BLACKBIRD SINGING

by R. S. Thomas

It seems wrong that out of this bird,
Black, bold, a suggestion of dark
Places about it, there yet should come
Such rich music, as though the notes'
Ore were changed to a rare metal
At one touch of that bright bill.

You have heard it often, alone at your desk
In a green April, your mind drawn
Away from its work by sweet disturbance
Of the mild evening outside your room.

A slow singer, but loading each phrase
With history's overtones, love, joy
And grief learned by his dark tribe
In other orchards and passed on
Instinctively as they are now,
But fresh always with new tears.

'It seems wrong . . .'. The poem opens with a discordant,
almost a grudging note. What has beauty to do with darkness,
or 'rich music' with an appearance so black and bold? The poet's
mood is tranquil and peaceful, amid the 'sweet disturbance/Of the
mild evening'. His first feeling on hearing the song is that good
and evil should be more sorted out, more segregated, than they

are in the blackbird. Yet we know at once that this feeling is a mistake, which the poet has recognised even before he expresses it. The bird has a 'bright bill', for all its dark and bold suggestions. 'One touch' of this bill turns its song to gold. The image is taken from alchemy, and there is indeed magic at work—the magic of experience, forcing upon us a more complex awareness of light and dark than simple innocence might wish.

The bird is a 'slow singer'; and like Keats's nightingale it takes on a universalised meaning for the listening poet. Keats, of course, moved from the real bird to a symbolic one; the song ceased to be that of one bird, and became the embodiment of lasting and eternal Beauty—a song that never was on land or sea. R. S. Thomas's movement of thought is rather different. In his poem, the bird remains a real bird in a real place, but touches off thoughts beyond itself. It is seen both as part of a dynasty—one representative of the long tribe of blackbirds that have led up to it, and to whom it is united by instinct—and also as an individual, re-enacting the experience of the tribe. Just because of this, however, it becomes a fitting symbol for human experience where darkness and rich music also co-exist, protest though we will, from our deep passion for serenity, 'It seems wrong . . .'. The blackbird becomes, in fact, a natural symbol. It releases the poet's imagination into profound if still simple reflections, but does this just because it is a real, and not an idealised bird.

In the third stanza the reference to history is important; it refers to the dynasty of blackbirds, and by implication to our human dynasty as well:

> A slow singer, but loading each phrase
> With history's overtones, love, joy,
> And grief learned by his dark tribe
> In other orchards and passed on
> Instinctively as they are now,
> But fresh always with new tears.

The suggestions are very concentrated but quite precise. R. S. Thomas is a poet to whom 'history's overtones' are inseparable from his visual imagination; he *sees* the past in the present, a living and shaping force at every point. In this he differs from Wordsworth, whose sense of Nature was wholly separate from his historical sense; he differs, indeed, from most 'nature' poets, including Edward Thomas, to whom in certain other ways he is somewhat akin. Many of his images are grounded in evolution, in the deep awareness that the individual belongs to its species just as the present belongs to the past. 'Instinct' is the filial bond between ourselves and Nature: the bond which unites our personal experience to the wisdom and suffering of the race. It is more deeply bred in us than 'experience', more close (perhaps) to the sources of poetry and religion as well; yet experience confirms it in our own lives and destinies. The song is old, but the tears of its singers are always new.

So what this third stanza offers is more complex, for all its ease, than the serenity behind that opening hesitation, 'It seems wrong'. It offers love, joy, grief in trinity; a vision in which darkness and rich music belong to one another, as opposite sides of the same coin. The poet has been attending to the bird, and in attending has imitated it—for is not art itself very often the turning of sorrow into beauty, an alchemy very close to that perceived in the bird? His vision is partly that of Shelley (also touched off by the song of a bird) 'Our sweetest songs are those that tell of saddest thought'. But it is stronger and more specific than Shelley's; it is a vision of the individual entering into a tragic inheritance, and finding it at once his own and not his own. The blackbird's grief is a common inheritance, 'learned by his dark tribe/In other orchards', but the experience lives only in individual birds, who realise the inheritance for themselves. One can scarcely imagine this particular perception of a tragic dynasty expressed with greater compression or tact. The blackbird is made to bear not one jot more symbolic significance than it can.

One feels that the poem springs from a genuine sense of the community of all living things, which enables the poet to identify himself with other forms of life without the least sense of artificiality or strain.

For the poet does not simply use the bird as an excuse for his reverie. In the fullest sense his poem is a celebration of the bird. One cannot fail to notice a very characteristic ambivalence, which is to be found in R. S. Thomas's poetry not only here, but wherever one looks. There is a blending of love and hate, attraction and repulsion in his feelings for all of the things that matter to him most—for Wales, for the hill farmer Iago Prytherch, for his own religious experience, indeed for himself. In this poem it is the blackbird which sets up this ambivalence, through its mingling of the beautiful with the dark. The poet's serenity is intruded upon by this apparent discord; but in accepting it he is moved towards a deeper awareness of life, where the springs of his own poetry are to be found.

In form 'A Blackbird Singing' is a variant of free verse, with four stressed syllables in each line. The diction is measured yet full of variety. The poem's content is so rounded and satisfying that we have almost an illusion of rhyme. In fact it is unrhymed like most of Thomas's poems, but we notice this with a distinct feeling of surprise.

The poem has, like many of R. S. Thomas's lyrics, the mark of greatness upon it. Its mingling of simplicity and profundity is of a kind rarely achieved, temptingly easy though the finished poem appears to be. Very naturally we think back, in seeking analogies for it, to George Herbert and even (despite an entire difference in temperament) to Blake—to the great touchstones in English poetry for very simple lyrics, which grow in stature and richness as we live with them.

17

AT GRASS *by Philip Larkin*

THE eye can hardly pick them out
From the cold shade they shelter in,
Till wind distresses tail and mane;
Then one crops grass, and moves about
—The other seeming to look on—
And stands anonymous again.

Yet fifteen years ago, perhaps
Two dozen distances sufficed
To fable them: faint afternoons
Of Cups and Stakes and Handicaps,
Whereby their names were artificed
To inlay faded, classic Junes—

Silks at the start: against the sky
Numbers and parasols: outside,
Squadrons of empty cars, and heat,
And littered grass: then the long cry
Hanging unhushed till it subside
To stop-press columns on the street.

Do memories plague their ears like flies?
They shake their heads. Dusk brims the shadows.
Summer by summer all stole away,
The starting-gates, the crowds and cries—
All but the unmolesting meadows.
Almanacked, their names live; they

Have slipped their names, and stand at ease,
Or gallop for what must be joy,
And not a fieldglass sees them home,
Or curious stop-watch prophesies:
Only the groom, and the groom's boy,
With bridles in the evening come.

The old racehorses in this poem are first seen lost in shadow,
almost undistinguishable until the wind moves a tail or mane.
Using only very simple words, Larkin invests this situation with
a richness of emotional effects. The horses seem to be fading into
death, their unique identities slipping back to the darkness from
which they came. We are reminded of the pathos of old age and
the swift passing of time. It is as if the horses were the shades of
all human ambitions and triumphs. They have left behind them
all that gave significance to their lives. Their movements have
no meaning; one *seems* to look at the other, but probably sees
nothing. No purpose gives them an identity, or rescues them
from anonymity. It is as if all existence proceeds in the same
direction, as time wastes away the shapes we have tried to make
out of our lives. In the last stanza of the poem, we are reminded
of the pleasure of freedom, as the racehorses stand at ease and
gallop for joy, but in the first stanza, words such as 'cold'
and 'distresses' make the horses seem pathetic in their retirement.

This poem uses imagery in a manner very different from that
of Yeats or Eliot. The horses are not, like Yeats's swan or Eliot's
rose, symbols that embody the poet's unique insights into the
nature of reality. Larkin thinks of himself not as a gifted seer,
but as a man speaking to men. In his view, the poet's uniqueness
lies mainly in his technical ability, his power to compose
sequences of words that express fully and adequately the human
situation. 'At Grass' is a reflective poem, carefully constructed,
and commenting in beautiful, dignified language on the penalties

and pleasures of retirement. It celebrates the mystery of the human lot. The condition of the old is sad, for the triumphs of their youth lie so many years behind; yet there is a certain joy in being no longer involved in a useless race for power. Of course, like any great poet, Larkin cannot reflect on the ordinary things of life, on transience and death, without imposing his own attitudes of mind. 'At Grass' expresses his resignation, his distrust of the energetic use of the will. But, above all, the poem is a simple lament about old age, describing experiences we can readily understand, and in which probably we will eventually participate.

Because he is not concerned to 'mime' his own unique apprehensions of reality, Larkin never uses free verse. He writes in traditional rhythms, metres, rhymes and syntax because his concern is to celebrate traditional feelings. 'At Grass' is a fine example of his technical ability. The simple words join together in a most distinctive, melancholy rhythm, and the octosyllabic lines, so carefully constructed, are particularly appropriate for this sad, resigned tone. The rhyme scheme, with its occasional variations such as the linking of 'in' and 'on' in the first stanza, gives an air of inevitability to the reflections of the poem.

The second stanza goes back into the past to describe the triumphs of the racehorses, but the mood remains the same. 'Two dozen distances' suggests the smallness of the actions that make fables, and the word 'faint' evokes nostalgia by reminding us that the afternoons are well in the past, now remembered only indistinctly. The last line recalls those old paintings of racehorses that often hang in a pub or commercial hotel. They always seem curiously unreal, and it is difficult to believe that the people and events actually existed. The stanza as a whole comments ironically on the way humans impose great meanings on their actions, for the words 'fable', 'artificed', and 'classic' (referring to the classic races—the Derby, etc.) recall the most important creations of man, even art itself, and make these seem ephemeral.

The third stanza describes the colour and vitality of the race-meeting, the silks of the jockeys, the numbers of the horses in their frames and the parasols of the ladies. But, typically, the viewpoint stays focussed on this energetic life for only two lines. We move to the abandoned car-park, whose empty cars and littered grass tell of picnics just completed. By making the shouts, as the race ends, into 'a long cry', pathos is introduced again. The cry moves outwards across the country, as newspapers headline the winner's name in stop-press columns. And newspaper fame is perhaps the most short-lived of all.

The fourth stanza begins with a slight change of tempo. By using nine syllables in the first three lines, Larkin slows down the movement, and so appropriately reintroduces his own reflections. The fourth line, with only eight syllables, has a quicker movement to suit the race-meeting, and this is contrasted with the fifth line, again with nine syllables, which re-imposes the melancholy feelings of the poem. In this stanza, the situation of the horses is not without rewards. Memories do not 'plague' them, nor are they 'molested' by the meadows. They have a freedom which humans can never achieve, but which at times seems desirable. They have escaped from the burden of memory, and from all the pressures of society. The last line has only seven syllables. 'Almanacked', a long word, suggesting dignity and pomp, is contrasted with the ending of the line. 'They' is an unusual word, short and lacking emphasis, with which to finish a stanza. After the heavy stresses of 'almanacked', 'they' slips the poem into a minor key, and into the concluding stanza.

The last stanza confirms this almost quietistic mood. The horses have escaped from their names. The impositions of society, which force purposes and categories upon us, are taken away. And for a moment, the horses have an ideal freedom. They use their powers as they please, and no one stands by to measure their attainment or to prophesy about the future. Only at the end of the day, the groom and his boy come with bridles to lead them home. The placing of the simple word 'come' at the very end of the poem suggests the inevitability of the horses' fate. As they are taken back to the stables, it is as if, as with all men, they are submitting to death.

18

THE CASUALTY *by Ted Hughes*

FARMERS in the fields, housewives behind steamed windows,
Watch the burning aircraft across the blue sky float,
As if a firefly and a spider fought,
Far above the trees, between the washing hung out.
They wait with interest for the evening news.

But already, in a brambled ditch, suddenly-smashed
Stems twitch. In the stubble a pheasant
Is craning every way in astonishment.
The hare that hops up, quizzical, hesitant,
Flattens ears and tears madly away and the wren warns.

Some, who saw fall, smoke beckons. They jostle above,
They peer down a sunbeam as if they expected there
A snake in the gloom of the brambles or a rare flower,—
See the grave of dead leaves heave suddenly, hear
It was a man fell out of the air alive,

Hear now his groans and senses groping. They rip
The slum of weeds, leaves, barbed coils; they raise
A body that as the breeze touches it glows,
Branding their hands on his bones. Now that he has
No spine, against heaped sheaves they prop him up,

Arrange his limbs in order, open his eye,
Then stand, helpless as ghosts. In a scene
Melting in the August noon, the burned man
Bulks closer greater flesh and blood than their own,
As suddenly the heart's beat shakes his body and the eye

Widens childishly. Sympathies
Fasten to the blood like flies. Here's no heart's more
Open or large than a fist clenched, and in there
Holding close complacency its most dear
Unscratchable diamond. The tears of their eyes

Too tender to let break, start to the edge
Of such horror close as mourners can,
Greedy to share all that is undergone,
Grimace, gasp, gesture of death. Till they look down
On the handkerchief at which his eye stares up.

The major theme in Ted Hughes's early poems is power; and
power thought of not morally or in time, but absolutely, in a
present which is often violent and self-destructive, but isolated
from motive or consequence, and so unmodified by the irony
which time confers. Violence is the occasion not for reflection
but for *being*; it is a guarantee of energy and life and most so,
paradoxically, when it knows itself in moments of captivity, pain
or death. In the poem called 'The Jaguar', the poet looks at the
caged beast, as it hurries 'enraged Through prison darkness after
the drills of its eyes', and finds victory in its untamed will:

> there's no cage to him
> More than to the visionary his cell.
> His stride is wildernesses of freedom.

Beast and visionary are linked in the triumph of will over
circumstance; in 'The Martyrdom Of Bishop Farrar' he goes
further, and finds triumph in a moment of martyrdom. The
flame 'shrivels sinew and chars bone', but the spirit rises superior
to suffering. The bishop's victory is one of pure stoicism, creating
in the flames a timeless moment of glory, which is the currency
of heroism, and so good coin long after his own flesh is con-
sumed:

His body's cold-kept miserdom of shrieks
He gave uncounted, while out of his eyes
  Out of his mouth, fire like a glory broke,
And smoke burned his sermons into the skies.

One is reminded here, as often in the other poems, of Yeats's 'Easter 1916'. Essentially ordinary men are taken, by one act of heroism consummated in death, out of the humdrum world of everyday into the lasting world of symbols. There is a constant striving in these poems towards moments of significance, moments of greatness that will last, as symbols if not as facts; towards ideal events more enduring than their agents, and triumphant as death itself.

In the poem we are concerned with here, 'The Casualty', the theme is also violent death; and though we are not certain that the dead man is a hero (planes burn out and crash even in peacetime) it is reasonable to suppose that he is. We are reminded of the Battle of Britain, and the particular heroisms of fighter-pilots. At the start, the doomed airman is caught into the loneliness of violent death. His burning aircraft removes him from the company of the indifferent living, who watch from below, into the company of the more meaningful dead. In falling 'out of the air alive' he becomes of unique significance. The price is immediate death, the breaking of his body beyond repair ('Now that he has No spine, against heaped leaves they prop him up'). Yet it is the living, confronted by his death, who stand 'helpless as ghosts', and the dead man, by virtue of his sudden death, who 'Bulks closer greater flesh and blood than their own'. The word 'alive', with its serious, non-ironic application to the dead man falling, enables death to take on its full ambivalence, as an event both terrible and glorious:

A snake in the gloom of the brambles or a rare flower.

This either/or in the fact of death is the dichotomy which the poet takes care not to resolve. It is by segregating the two possibilities, and stopping them from meeting, that he is enabled to enter into both as he does: exploring the 'rare flower' in particular, undiverted by that ironic no-man's-land between the either/or where most contemporary poets are to be found.

The attitudes of the human and animal witnesses to the accident are contrasted throughout. The 'Farmers in the fields, housewives behind steamed windows' are on the whole indifferent. It is not that they are wicked, but simply that they fail in imagination. The 'washing hung out' (line 4) places the episode in a perspective of ordinary domestic curiosity. The 'interest' with which the evening news is awaited is that ordinary, rather ghoulish interest we have in disaster: not strong enough to lead to action, but strong enough to increase our own prestige slightly, as the witnesses of great events. In the second stanza, the animal observers react more strongly and decisively. Ted Hughes watches them with that close attention and respect which characterises his approach to animals—

> In the stubble a pheasant
> Is craning every way in astonishment.
> The hare that hops up, quizzical, hesitant,
> Flattens ears and tears madly away and the wren warns . . .

This is closely and faithfully observed and is by no means sentimental. The animals are motivated by fear of a threat they do not fully understand; they are too alien to the dying airman to care for him, but too alien also to share the curiously unsatisfactory responses of his fellow men. In the fourth stanza, the physical horror of death is fully brought home to us in pithy, mostly monosyllabic words, which enact the last moments of twitching agony:

> Hear now his groans and senses groping. They rip
> The slum of weeds, leaves, barbed coils; they raise
> A body that as the breeze touches it glows,
> Branding their hands on his bones.

And when human observers enter again, it is in a more positively unpleasant way than before. They come now as a crowd to watch an accident:

> Greedy to share all that is undergone,
> Grimace, gasp, gesture of death.

This kind of participation is certainly vicarious and very possibly sadistic. The very feelings of the onlookers are described in terms of greed and the parasitic; 'Sympathies/Fasten to their blood like flies.' At the end, the watching crowd is not only as 'helpless' as ghosts, but also as insubstantial. The dead man remains 'closer greater flesh and blood'—a grim paradox, in which the very nature of heroism seems to be caught.

The poem is marked by its visual clarity, and its highly distinctive tone; there is no explicit moral, but we are made to see, and therefore to judge, with quite remarkable force. In actual form, it is fairly free verse: there are five stresses in each line, but no metrical norm; the last words in the three central lines of each stanza are slightly linked in that they end with the same consonant sound; there is much alliteration, but not of a systematic kind. The poem's concreteness and sharpness comes from visual clarity, compression, intensity of tone (there is a kind of violence of controlled perception), and from the remarkable vigour of vocabulary and syntax. Its imagery is original and striking ('A snake in the gloom of the brambles or a rare flower', 'The slum of weeds, leaves, barbed coils') but its observation, both of humans and animals, has the force of unanswerable truth.

In 'Famous Poet', Ted Hughes describes the poet himself as an onlooker on life. The poet tries to 'concoct The old heroic bang' from the deeds of others, but is himself 'wrecked' in the attempt, and ends not united with his object, but exhausted and diminished, 'like a badly hurt man, half life-size'. The human ghosts in this poem are not dissimilar. Is it, perhaps, that the irony which Ted Hughes resolutely keeps out of heroic events he cannot wholly exclude from people? Events partake of eternity, as poems do; but people, and poets, share the doom of a turning world.

19

CONSIDERING THE SNAIL

by Thom Gunn

THE snail pushes through a green
night, for the grass is heavy
with water and meets over
the bright path he makes, where rain
has darkened the earth's dark. He
moves in a wood of desire,

pale antlers barely stirring
as he hunts. I cannot tell
what power is at work, drenched there
with purpose, knowing nothing.
What is a snail's fury? All
I think is that if later

I parted the blades above
the tunnel and saw the thin
trail of broken white across
litter, I would never have
imagined the slow passion
to that deliberate progress.

This is a most unusual poem. At a first, quick glance it might
seem just a vivid, descriptive poem. But soon we have to acknowledge that the deliberate rhythms create a most original music,
and that the lucid, muscular language has a compelling power.
How does this description of a snail become so charged with

meaning? This seems a form of free verse, but it is very different from the experimental poetry of Eliot, Lawrence and Pound, and the total effect is one of great lucidity and control. What new technique of versification is being used? This is one of Thom Gunn's most recent poems. It is undoubtedly a great poem, and a brilliant experiment in a new form. Still only in his early thirties, Gunn promises to be one of the most courageous and exceptional poets of his times.

Thom Gunn first became known as a poet when he was still an undergraduate at Cambridge in the early 1950's. The Fantasy Press published his first pamphlet of verse before he graduated, and shortly afterwards in 1954 his first volume, *Fighting Terms*. Two more books of verse have followed, *The Sense of Movement* (1957) and *My Sad Captains* (1961). For many years now he has been teaching in California, though he still makes frequent visits to this country. He likes the American landscape because it is bare, and lacks the rich historical associations of England. In 'Flying Above California', he describes the Pacific coastline:

> on fogless days by the Pacific,
> there is a cold hard light without break
>
> that reveals merely what is—no more
> and no less. That limiting candour,
>
> that accuracy of the beaches,
> is part of the ultimate richness.

This unusual preference for clear, uncomplicated vistas derives from Gunn's philosophical questionings, and these underlie the strength of a poem such as 'Considering the Snail'. He is very much out of sympathy with the indecisions and uncertainties of a poet such as Philip Larkin. He has a hate, almost a contempt, for people who are afraid to choose, for the half-hearted and the timid. He firmly asserts the heroism of the romantic will. Such attitudes might seem untypical of our times, and certainly most rare among academics; but Gunn's energetic self-sufficiency defines itself in very contemporary terms. He does not pretend that he understands the consequences of his actions or their ultimate meanings. In a world of mystery and uncertainty, he is determined to act, to choose, even though the results may be beyond his comprehension. In an admirable article in *The Critical Quarterly* (Vol. 3, No. 4), G. S. Fraser argues that the tough, young leather-jacketed motor-cyclists, figures who appear repeatedly in Gunn's verse, are most suitable symbols for his attitude to life. The restless energy of the motor-cyclist expresses itself in violent movement with no clear purpose. He joys in being on the move, and does not concern himself with precise destinations. This represents Gunn's own conception of moral choice. He asserts the values of will even though his actions appear to have no social purpose. John Mander has said of Gunn that he is living in a state of 'existential pre-commitment.' At times he appears uncompromisingly ruthless. Occasionally, however, his poise seems achieved with difficulty, and in recent poems there have been some considerable doubts. In 'My Sad Captains', the last poem in his recent volume, he sees his heroes cloaked in darkness. They are men who 'lived only to renew the wasteful force they spent with each hot convulsion', but in this poem the firm assertions conflict with a feeling of ultimate pathos.

Ted Hughes expresses violence in the actions of a hawk, a jaguar or a pike. Thom Gunn does not usually write about animals or birds, and it has been suggested that 'Considering the Snail' is a deliberate parody of Hughes. Like Hughes, Gunn observes very closely, and the language mimes the consciousness of the snail. The words 'green night' and 'heavy with water' make us almost apprehend the snail's sensuous awareness of the sodden grass through which he pushes. But the attitudes expressed in the poem are uniquely those of Gunn himself. He presents the movement of the snail, 'the slow passion' of 'that deliberate progress' with a tone of surprise, even admiration. In the first line, 'pushes' is very strongly emphasised, and throughout the poem we feel the strong will of the snail, 'drenched there with purpose'. This concentrated energy is a kind of value that Gunn reveres. The snail makes a 'bright path', a 'thin trail of broken white across litter.' With unswerving determination, he moves on direct to his goal. But a snail is a small, slimy creature, and Gunn deliberately chooses such an image to embody the values of determination and will. The 'pale antlers barely stirring' frighten us with the mystery of life, so delicately constructed and yet linked to so blind a purpose. As in 'My Sad Captains', Gunn is concerned with the apparent meaninglessness of so much perseverance and resolution. 'What is a snail's fury?' Heroic postures begin no longer to satisfy, and one wonders whether Gunn is moving towards some major change of attitude. Are the choices of human beings as blind and limited as those of a snail? In the first stanza, the images convey the darkness in which we all live, 'knowing nothing'. The 'green night', 'wood of desire' and the earth darkened by rain symbolise the nightmare blackness that surrounds the modern consciousness. What meanings can we find? Gunn admits that he has no explanations: 'I cannot tell what power is at work . . .' But the poem does not end with complete uncertainty. If, like some God, he parted the blades above the tunnel, and looked at the signs of past activity, he would never have imagined the passions involved. So the poem, with its mixture of the heroic and the mock heroic, ends by celebrating the deliberate progress of the snail.

The book, *My Sad Captains*, is divided into two sections. The first part includes poems in traditional metres, but the second is devoted to poems in 'syllabic' metre. Of these 'Considering the Snail' is one of the best examples. Syllabic metre is new in English verse, and has roused considerable controversy. To many readers, it appears like arbitrarily divided prose, and criticisms have often been the same as those directed at free verse. Syllabic metre has been used successfully in America by Marianne Moore, William Carlos Williams and W. H. Auden. A full account is given in a review of *My Sad Captains* in *The Times Literary Supplement*, September 29, 1961. Each line has a certain number of fixed syllables, usually six, seven or nine, with, in general, two main stresses and one or two secondary stresses, all of which may occur at any point in the line. The line is usually read at an even and level pace, with a pause—however slight—at the end of each line even where in iambic metre there would be enjambment. The reviewer in *The Times Literary Supplement* argues that in ordinary American speech there is not the contrast between long and short vowels, nor the variation of stress and pitch there is in standard Southern English speech. Syllabic metre, therefore, is particularly successful in imposing form on American conversational idioms. Richard Murphy was one of the first English poets to experiment in this form, and his verses produced a vigorous controversy published under the heading, 'The Muse in Chains', in *The Times Literary Supplement* in 1960. In a letter of June 17, Murphy argued:

> The poet's problem is to find a metre which is strong enough to control the rhythmical resources inherent in our language, yet free enough to allow him to use that language as it is spoken today. Free verse is not a metre, yet the poet needs freedom above all to overcome the old echoes, the old attitudes that the iambic pentameter will always retain, together with the haunting influence of all its great lines. Yet he does not want complete freedom from metre, for then he must lose all musical emotional power which can only be generated by a language on which metre, meaning 'measure', has been imposed, and a speech in which the metrical scale is subtly and inherently involved.

This raises many problems, and free verse has already been discussed in our introduction. Syllabic metre is an attempt to impose new formal structures on modern conversational rhythms. In 'Considering the Snail', Gunn creates a new and subtle relationship between form and the speaking voice. If this is read as straight prose, its characteristic rhythm is completely lost. The pause at the end of the line imposes on the words a deliberation of tone which most fittingly reflects the movement of the snail. This slow, heavy movement is also enforced by the placing of two stressed syllables together. In 'snail pushes', 'green night', 'bright path', 'earth's dark', 'drenched there', and 'slow passions', the two emphasised syllables give a sense of deliberate, snail-like progress. The careful arrangement of each line into seven syllables gives a sense of order and control. Only at the beginning of the third stanza is there a lighter movement, and this is introduced to contrast with the conclusion of the poem. The perseverance of the snail is firmly asserted, and the last line, with eight syllables, fittingly rounds off the poem. The poem, 'My Sad Captains', has a different music: use of lightly stressed words such as 'in', 'and', 'a', and 'to' at the end of the seven syllable line creates a most original tone of pathos. These poems in the second section of *My Sad Captains* have a beautiful, subtle music, and offer new technical possibilities to the modern writer.

20

ON THE DEATH
OF A MURDERER

by John Wain

'ONE day Vera showed us a photograph of some local Gestapo men which had come into her hands. The photograph had been taken when they were in the country outside Prague for a day's holiday. The young men were ranged in two rows in their neat uniforms, and they stared out at us with professionally menacing but unhappy eyes from that recent past now dead.

'. . . After the relief of Prague these young men were hunted through the countryside, Vera told us, like wild game, and all of them taken and killed.'

Edwin Muir, *Autobiography*

Over the hill the city lights leaped up.
But there in the fields the quiet dusk folds down.
A man lies in a ditch.He listens hard.
His own fast breathing is the biggest sound
But through it, coming nearer, he hears another:
The voices of his hunters, coming nearer.

They are coming, and he can run no further.

He was born in a Germany thrashing like a fish
On a gravel towpath beating out its life.
As a child, something they called the Blockade
Nearly strangled him with impersonal cold fingers.

Clever doctors saved his life. The Blockade receded,
He hopped in the Berlin streets like a cool sparrow.
His wise friends showed him a quick way to earn
Pocket-money: while English schoolboys chalked
Dirty words and sniggered behind desk-lids,
He learnt the things the words meant; his pockets
Filled up with change and his heart jingled with hate.

Now his hate has jingled in the ears of Europe.
He has taught them to know the refusal of pity.
His life is nearly over; only the darkness
Covers him as his pursuers cry over the fields.
In a moment they will tear him to pieces.
He was sick of the things that went with the dirty words:
Sick of the pocket-money and the windy street.
Then the uniforms came. They said to him: *Be strong*

When he was fifteen, he had a gun.
He had forgotten the Blockade and the pocket-money,
Except on nights when he could not sleep: his gun
Was a friend, but when they gave him a whip
He loved that better still. *Be strong!* He cried.
The speeches were made, the leaves fell, it was war.
To smashed Prague his gun and his whip led him in time.
There, he learnt the delight of refusing pity.

Did he never wonder about those he murdered?
Never feel curious about the severe light
That flamed in their irises as they lay dying?
Apparently not. His duty took all his care.
He fed his starving heart with cruelty
Till it got sick and died. His masters applauded.
Once, he dragged off a man's lower jaw.

Now they are coming nearer over the fields.
It is like the Blockade, only worse. He will die.
They have taken away his whip and gun.

But let us watch the scene with a true eye,
Arrest your pen, hurrying chronicler.
Do you take this for a simple act: the mere
Crushing of a pest that crawled on the world's hide?
Look again: is there not an ironic light
In the fiery sky that rings his desperate head?

He will die, this cursed man. The first pursuer
Is here. The darkness is ready to give him up.
He has, at most, a hundred breaths to draw.
But what of the cunning devil that jerked his strings?
Is that one idle, now that the strings are cut?

The man's body will rot under lime, and that soon.
But the parades have taught his uniform to march.
The hunters close in: do they feel the danger?
When they wrench his body to pieces, will they hear
A sigh as his spirit is sucked into the air
That they must breathe? And will his uniform
March on, march on, across Europe? Will their children
Hop in the streets like cool sparrows, and draw
His spirit into their hopeful lungs? Will
Their hearts jingle with hate? And who shall save them
If after all the years and all the deaths
They find a world still pitiless, a street
Where no grass of love grows over the hard stones?

'On the Death of a Murderer' is a narrative poem, describing the death of a young man. It could scarcely be called a blank verse poem, since the metre is only very approximately iambic. Perhaps all the lines could just about be scanned in terms of iambic pentametres (the one exception is 'When he was fifteen he had a gun'), but this would require a frequent use of feminine endings and a resolute blind-eye to the meaning. In fact, the rhythms of the speaking voice shift with the sense, in a manner more usual in free verse than in even the loosest variant of blank verse. The syntax and grammar are straightforward, and the voice we hear is very obviously the poet's own. The imagery is vivid and sensitive without being original. It refers to everyday sights and sounds which we are made to feel, however, with more than usual clarity—a fish that has just been caught, a small boy playing hop-scotch, a column of uniformed soldiers marching along. John Wain's sympathy with the hooked fish is clearly instinctive:

> He was born in a Germany thrashing like a fish
> On a gravel towpath beating out its life.

The fish symbolises the plight of human victims (in this case all Germany), but it receives sympathy in its own right. Some readers may think this sentimental, yet many great writers have believed that kindness even to the lowest orders of creation is part of the dignity of man. We are conscious of the poet's compassion in the beautiful image of the young boy, still uncorrupted, hopping 'in the Berlin streets like a cool sparrow' (an image which recurs at the end, with the whole force of the poem's cyclical development behind it). But in other parts of the poem the poet deliberately withholds his own emotional colouring, so that we can look ourselves with a 'true eye'. The section which deals with the dying Nazi's own cruelties is dispassionate without being detached: we are made to feel its horror, but simple revulsion is not the chief emotion that the poet wants of us:

> Did he never wonder about those he murdered?
> Never feel curious about the severe light
> That flamed in their irises as they lay dying?
> Apparently not. His duty took all his care.
> He fed his starving heart with cruelty
> Till it got sick and died. His masters applauded.
> Once, he dragged off a man's lower jaw.

What we are most conscious of here is a lucidity of compassionate attention to a suffering world; it is attention of the kind which characterises many of Wain's best poems, 'A Song about Major Eatherley' for instance, and the poem which begins 'Like a deaf man meshed in his endless silence'. The detachment is not a suspension of feeling, but a willingness to let the situation speak directly to us; the poet's part is to achieve telling articulation, and a careful arrangement of facts. By this means, he does not prevent us from feeling horror: he ensures, however, that our horror will not rest in the simple condemnation of one man we know to be bad.

In conception this is a very daring poem, with strategy more carefully thought out than we might at first suppose. The title tells us that the hunted young man is a murderer, and the prose note (if we read it first) tells us what kind of a murderer he is. But the poem itself opens with the young man as a victim: we are made to feel his own fear as the hunters draw near, so that some sympathy with him is established before we fully understand who he is. In the second section, the poet goes on to explain the causes of his wickedness. The Nazi is a victim not only in his death, but in his life. Born in a victimised country, attacked by the cruelly impersonal Blockade (which he did nothing to deserve, but had to suffer), later corrupted by more personal temptations, he is scarcely the master of his fate. When, because of this background, his heart is dead, it is easy for power to come as a form of total corruption; for him to become in a true sense the scourge of Europe:

> Now his hate has jingled in the ears of Europe.
> He has taught them to know the refusal of pity . . .

The poet's purpose here must be carefully observed. He is not whitewashing the dead Nazi, or trying to gain sympathy for his actual deeds: on the contrary, in the next section, the man's cruelties are described with revulsion. Nor is he suggesting that

the Nazi was wholly the victim of his environment and unable
to help himself, for this would be a kind of determinism which
the very conception of the poem denies. What we are made to
see about the Nazi is that he is not the originator of cruelty, but
one link in its chain. He exists in a world that to some degree
caused him, and of which he is to that same degree the true
reflection. The Nazi himself will die, and justly:

> He will die, this cursed man . . .
> The man's body will rot under lime, and that soon . . .

But the word 'cursed' faces two ways: in the obvious sense it is
a synonym for 'vile', but in its older sense it suggests the victim
of a curse. The Nazi's cruelty is the central link in a chain which
started before he was corrupt, and which continues when he
himself is hunted. His very death is a kind of poetic justice that
defeats the larger civilised values it appears to serve. What Wain
has done is to enforce 'the refusal of pity' upon us as a disease;
and a disease not of one man only, but of the whole age in which
his drama has its part. In a remarkable image, he sees the dying
man's 'spirit' sucked into the general air, and breathed in by
other youngsters who, still uncorrupt, hop in the cool streets
like sparrows. The Nazi 'dragged off a man's jaw', but is himself
to suffer the avengers who 'wrench his body to pieces'. Just as
his wickedness was in some sense a reflection of his age, or even
its punishment, so his death continues the cycle of vengeance
and violence by which he was made. The poem's effect is to make
us fearful rather than glad when justice is done. A poem about
justice alone would be far too easy, as we are told:

> But let us watch the scene with a true eye.
> Arrest your pen, hurrying chronicler.
> Do you take this for a simple act: the mere
> Crushing of a pest that crawled on the world's hide?
> Look again: is there not an ironic light
> In the fiery sky that rings his desperate head?

What is easier for us than to hate an enemy? We have every reason to do so, and in wartime it might seem the only attitude we could adopt. But can we go on from here to pity the enemy too? And from pity, can we come to see ourselves as part of a cycle of suffering which justice and hatred can perpetuate, but never bring to an end? For in hating, we capture his own disease, 'the delight in refusing pity'; and this disease, well understood, is not his peculiar flaw, but an infection in the cycle of suffering and bloodshed itself. The old Greek tragedies often centred on such cycles, where revenge seemed fated to carry doom from one generation to another, unless some greater law were discovered to take its place. John Wain looks here at our twentieth-century cycle and captures it as its most sensitive and challenging point. The pest itself is trapped, and the trappers make themselves and their children in its very image. As readers we are challenged by understanding and pity, not by the stock responses and complacencies of revenge.

This is why the poet makes us see the dead man as hunted before we see him as hunter, and why our very proper detestation of him leads towards, not away from, the wider issues his fate involves. A 'true eye' will see not only a hated object, but a suffering man; it will see not only evil but the causes of evil, which are deeply rooted in ourselves.

The poem, therefore, is organised in terms of its meaning; its imagery is compassionate, but its structure is a challenge to our intelligence and understanding as well as to our feeling. We see that the 'delight in refusing pity' is one of the permanent wrong turnings for the human race; we see that we are all tainted, and that because we are tainted we should seek not revenge, but a return to civilised values.

Whereas many modern poets evoke cruelty all too casually, Wain does so as part of a humane purpose. He does not want to turn our stomachs, but to influence our minds. The poem relies upon the civilised values we are still supposed to share. What is offered is not ambivalence, but a deepening insight into an evil, like ripples widening from a stone cast into a pool. We may end with a different judgement from that we started with, but if so, the poem has merely directed us to a response more complex and fruitful than simple disgust.

The poem has many 'memorable' lines. It ends with a beautiful return to earlier images, which carry the whole weight of the understanding the poem exists to achieve:

> And will his uniform
> March on, march on, across Europe? Will their children
> Hop in the streets like cool sparrows, and draw
> His spirit into their hopeful lungs? Will
> Their hearts jingle with hate? And who shall save them
> If after all the years and all the deaths
> They find a world still pitiless, a street
> Where no grass of love grows over the hard stones?

Only in the last line is the word towards which everything leads allowed to appear.

SHORT BIOGRAPHIES

AUDEN, WYSTAN HUGH. Born 1907, educated Gresham's School, Holt and Christ Church, Oxford. Associate Professor of English Literature, Ann Arbor University, Michigan; Guggenheim Research Fellowship, 1942; Professor of Poetry at Oxford, 1956-61; King George's Gold Medal for poetry, 1937. Lives in U.S.A., Member American Academy of Arts and Letters, 1954; Hon. President, Associated Societies of Edinburgh University.

DAY LEWIS, CECIL. Born 1904, educated Sherborne School and Wadham College, Oxford. Ministry of Information, 1941-46; Clark Lecturer, Trinity College, Cambridge, 1946; Professor of Poetry at Oxford, 1951-56; C.B.E., 1950. Also writes detective stories under the name of Nicholas Blake, and is a Director of Chatto and Windus.

DE LA MARE, WALTER. Born 1873, educated St. Pauls' Cathedral School. For some years followed a business career in London. C.H., 1948, O.M., 1953. Died 1956.

ELIOT, THOMAS STEARNS. Born 1888; educated Harvard University, the Sorbonne and Merton College, Oxford. Clark Lecturer, Trinity College, Cambridge, 1926; Charles Norton Professor of Poetry at Harvard, 1932-33; President of the Classical Association, 1943; Nobel Prize for Literature, 1948. He also edited *Criterion*, became an Officer de la Légion d'Honneur, and is a Director of Faber and Faber. Awarded the O.M. in 1948.

GRAVES, ROBERT. Born 1895, educated Charterhouse and St. John's College, Oxford. Served in France with Royal Welch Fusiliers. Professor of English Literature, Egyptian University, 1926; Clark Lecturer at Trinity College, Cambridge, 1954;

Professor of Poetry at Oxford since 1961; lives in Majorca.

GUNN, THOM. Born 1929, educated at Trinity College, Cambridge, since which he has lived mainly in the U.S.A.

HARDY, THOMAS. Born 1840, at Upper Bockhampton near Dorchester. In early life practised architecture. Became famous as a novelist, but ceased to write novels after *Jude The Obscure* (1895). Wrote an epic-drama *The Dynasts* (1904-8). Many of his finest poems were written in the present century. Died 1928.

HUGHES, TED. Born 1930, educated Mexborough Grammar School and Pembroke College, Cambridge. *The Hawk In The Rain* (1957), won the First Publication Award in an Anglo-American contest sponsored by the New York City Poetry Centre and judged by W. H. Auden, Stephen Spender and Marianne Moore. Won the Hawthornden Prize for Literature, 1961.

LARKIN, PHILIP. Born 1922, educated King Henry VIII School, Coventry and St. John's College, Oxford. Is now Librarian in the University of Hull.

LAWRENCE, D. H. Born 1885, educated at Nottingham High School and Nottingham University. Was a schoolmaster at Croydon until 1911, after which he devoted himself to writing. In 1914 he married Frieda von Richthofen. Like Hardy, he was better known as a novelist than as a poet, though his poems are among the best of the early years of this century. Died 1930.

MACNEICE, LOUIS. Born 1907, Belfast; educated Marlborough and Merton College, Oxford; Lectured in Classics at University of Birmingham, 1930-36, and in Greek at Bedford College, London, 1936-40. Has since worked for the B.B.C. Was Director of the British Institute, Athens, 1950; C.B.E., 1958.

MUIR, EDWIN. Born 1887, educated Kirkwall Burgh School, Orkney. Clerk in Glasgow, and later journalist, translator, author. Director of the British Institute of Rome, 1949;

Warden of Newbattle Abbey College, Dalkeith, 1950-55; Charles Eliot Norton Professor of Poetry at Harvard, 1955-56; Visiting Winston Churchill Professor at Bristol, 1958. Translated Kafka's *The Castle* and *The Trial* (with Willa Muir). C.B.E., 1953; died 1958.

OWEN, WILFRED. Born 1893, Oswestry; educated Birkenhead Institute and London University. He won the Military Cross during the First World War, and was killed in action in 1918, a week before the Armistice.

ROBERTS, MICHAEL. Born 1902; educated Bournemouth School, King's College, London, and Trinity College, Cambridge. Science Master, Royal Grammar School, Newcastle-upon-Tyne; European Service, B.B.C., 1941-45; Principal of the College of St. Mark and St. John, Chelsea from 1945; edited *The Faber Book of Modern Verse*, 1936; died 1948.

SPENDER, STEPHEN. Born 1909; educated University College School and University College, Oxford. Co-editor of *Horizon*, 1939-41; Counsellor, Section of Letters UNESCO, 1947; Co-editor of *Encounter* since 1953. Elliston Chair of Poetry, Cincinnati, 1953; Beckman Professor, California, 1959.

THOMAS, DYLAN. Born 1914 in Wales; educated Swansea Grammar School. For a time was reporter for the *South Wales Evening Post*; later writer and broadcaster. His play for broadcasting *Under Milk Wood* was produced in the early fifties, and later successfully adapted to the stage. Died 1953.

THOMAS, EDWARD. Born 1878, in London, of Welsh parents; educated St. Paul's, and Lincoln College, Oxford. He was a writer all his life, but became a poet only towards the end of it. He was killed in 1917.

THOMAS, RONALD STUART. Born 1913; educated University of Wales and St. Michael's College, Llandaff. Ordained deacon, 1936, priest, 1937. Rector of Manafon, 1942-54, Vicar of St. Michael's, Eglwysfach, since 1954.

WAIN, JOHN. Born 1925; educated The High School, Newcastle-under-Lyme and St. John's College, Oxford. Lecturer in English Literature at Reading, 1947-55; Director of the Festival of Poetry at the Mermaid, 1961.

YEATS, W. B. Born 1865, in Dublin, of predominantly Irish Protestant origin. Educated in London and at the High School and Metropolitan School of Art, Dublin. Settled in London, moving in literary, aesthetic, theosophical and spiritualist circles, but remained very much an Irish patriot at heart. He organised literary circles among the Fenians in Ireland; with the aid of Lady Gregory he produced *The Countess Cathleen* in Dublin (1899) and subsequently established the Abbey Theatre as a national institution. Nobel Prize for Literature, 1923; Senator, Irish Free State, 1922-28. Died 1939.

SUGGESTIONS FOR
FURTHER READING

This is not a comprehensive list of all books of poems and works of criticism. It is intended as a guide for the student and general reader, and makes no claim to scholarly completeness.

1. ANTHOLOGIES

Roberts, Michael, ed. *The Faber Book of Modern Verse.*

Heath-Stubbs, John and Wright, David, ed. *The Faber Book of Twentieth-Century Verse.*

Allott, Kenneth, ed. *The Penguin Book of Contemporary Verse*, Penguin Books.

Alvarez, A., ed. *The New Poetry*, Penguin Books.

2. BOOKS OF VERSE BY INDIVIDUAL POETS

Auden, W. H., *Collected Shorter Poems*, Faber and Faber, 1950; *For the Time Being*, Faber and Faber, 1945; *The Age of Anxiety*, Faber and Faber, 1948; *Nones*, Faber and Faber, 1952; *The Shield of Achilles*, Faber and Faber, 1955; *Homage to Clio*, Faber and Faber, 1960.

Day Lewis, C., *Collected Poems*, Jonathan Cape, 1954.

De la Mare, Walter, *Collected Poems*, Faber and Faber, 1942.

Eliot, T. S., *Collected Poems 1909-1935*, Faber and Faber, 1936; *Four Quartets*, Faber and Faber, 1944.

Graves, Robert, *Collected Poems 1959*, Cassell, 1959; *More Poems 1961*, Cassell, 1961; *New Poems 1962*, Cassell, 1962; *Selected Poetry and Prose*, chosen, introduced and annotated by James Reeves, Hutchinson Educational, 1961.

Gunn, Thom, *Fighting Terms* (reissued), Faber and Faber, 1962; *The Sense of Movement*, Faber and Faber, 1959; *My Sad Captains*, Faber and Faber, 1961.

Hardy, Thomas, *Collected Poems*, Macmillan, 1960.

Hughes, Ted, *The Hawk in the Rain*, Faber and Faber, 1957; *Lupercal*, Faber and Faber, 1960.

Larkin, Philip, *The Less Deceived*, The Marvell Press, 1955.

Lawrence, D. H., *The Complete Poems*, Heinemann, 1957.

MacNeice, Louis, *Collected Poems, 1925-1948*, Faber and Faber, 1949; *Visitations*, Faber and Faber, 1957.

Muir, Edwin, *Collected Poems, 1921-1958*, Faber and Faber, 1960.

Owen, Wilfred, *The Poems of Wilfred Owen*, edited by Edmund Blunden, The Phoenix Library, Chatto and Windus, 1933.

Roberts, Michael, *Collected Poems*, Faber and Faber, 1958.

Spender, Stephen, *Collected Poems, 1928-1953*, Faber and Faber, 1955.

Thomas, Dylan, *Collected Poems, 1934-1952*, J. M. Dent and Sons, 1952.

Thomas, Edward, *Collected Poems*, Faber and Faber, 1936.

Thomas, R. S., *Song at the Year's Turning*, Hart-Davis, 1955; *Poetry for Supper*, Hart-Davis, 1958; *Tares*, Hart-Davis, 1961.

Wain, John, *A Word Carved on a Sill*, Routledge and Kegan Paul, 1956; *Weep Before God*, Macmillan, 1961.

Yeats, W. B., *Collected Poems*, Macmillan, 1950.

3. CRITICISM

Brown, Douglas, *Thomas Hardy*, Longmans, 1954.

Butter, P. H., *Edwin Muir* (Writers and Critics) Oliver and Boyd, 1962.

Coombes, Henry, *Edward Thomas*, Chatto and Windus, 1956.

Cox, C. B., 'Philip Larkin', *The Critical Quarterly*, Vol. I, No. 1, 1959.

Daiches, David, *The Present Age*, The Cresset Press, 1958.

Davie, Donald, *Articulate Energy*, Routledge and Kegan Paul, 1955.

Dyson, A. E., 'Ted Hughes', *The Critical Quarterly*, Vol. I, No. 3, 1959.

Eliot, T. S., *Selected Essays*, Faber and Faber, 1932.

Ellmann, Richard, *Yeats, the Man and the Masks*, Macmillan, 1949; *The Identity of Yeats*, Macmillan, 1954.

Empson, William, *Seven Types of Ambiguity*, Chatto and Windus, 1930.

Fraser, G. S., 'The Poetry of Thom Gunn', *The Critical Quarterly*, Vol. III, No. 4, 1961.

Gardner, Helen, *The Art of T. S. Eliot*, Cresset Press, 1949; *The Business of Criticism*, Oxford University Press, 1959; 'The Academic Study of English Literature', *The Critical Quarterly*, Vol. I, No. 2, 1959.

Gaskell, Ronald, 'The Poetry of Robert Graves', *The Critical Quarterly*, Vol. III, No. 3, 1961.

Hoggart, Richard, *Auden: An Introductory Essay*, Chatto and Windus, 1951.

Hopkins, Kenneth, *Walter de la Mare* (Writers and their Work), Longmans, 1953.

Hough, Graham, *The Last Romantics* (on Yeats), Duckworth, 1949; *The Dark Sun* (on D. H. Lawrence), Duckworth, 1956; *Image and Experience*, Duckworth, 1960.

Kenner, Hugh, *The Invisible Poet: T. S. Eliot*, W. H. Allen, 1960.

Kermode, Frank, *Romantic Image*, Routledge and Kegan Paul, 1957.

Leavis, F. R., *D. H. Lawrence*, Chatto and Windus, 1955.

Lerner, Laurence, *The Truest Poetry*, Hamish Hamilton, 1960.

Lewis, C. S., *An Experiment in Criticism*, Cambridge University Press, 1961.

Matthiessen, F. O., *The Achievement of T. S. Eliot*, Oxford University Press, 3rd ed., 1958.

Merchant, W. Moelwyn, 'R. S. Thomas', *The Critical Quarterly*, Vol. II, No. 4, 1960.

Pinto, V. de S., 'Poet Without A Mask', *The Critical Quarterly*, Vol. III, No. 1, 1961.

Rajan, B., ed. *T. S. Eliot: a study of his writing by several hands*, Dobson, 1947.

Richards, I. A., *Practical Criticism*, Routledge and Kegan Paul, 1929.

Spender, Stephen, *The Struggle of the Modern*, Hamish Hamilton, 1963.

Welland, D. S. R., *Wilfred Owen: a critical study*, Chatto and Windus, 1960.